Betty Crocker

dinner made easy with

Rotisserie
Chicken

Betty Crocker

dinner made easy with
Rotisserie Chicken

BUILD A MEAL
Tonight!

WILEY

Wiley Publishing, Inc.

Library of Congress Cataloging-in-Publication Data:

Betty Crocker dinner made easy with rotisserie chicken : build a meal tonight.— 1st ed.

    p. cm.

Includes index.

ISBN 0-7645-7088-9 (pbk. : alk. paper)

1. Cookery (Chicken) 2. Roasting (Cookery) I. Crocker, Betty.

TX750.5.C45B49 2005

641.6'65—dc22

2004011939

Manufactured in the United States of America

10 9 8 7 6 5 4 3 2

Front cover photos: Easy Chicken Fajitas (page 114) and Chicken Enchilada Lasagna Bundles (page 150). Back cover photo: Adobe Chicken Wrap (page 104).

Photos on page 5 and 6: Vegetable-Chicken Stir-Fry (page 210) and Adobe Chicken Wrap (page 104), respectively.

General Mills, Inc.

DIRECTOR, BOOK AND ONLINE PUBLISHING: Kim Walter

MANAGER, BOOK PUBLISHING: Lois L. Tlusty

EDITOR: Lois L. Tlusty

RECIPE DEVELOPMENT AND TESTING: Betty Crocker Kitchens

FOOD STYLING: Betty Crocker Kitchens

PHOTOGRAPHY: General Mills Photo Studios

Wiley Publishing, Inc.

PUBLISHER: Natalie Chapman

EXECUTIVE EDITOR: Anne Ficklen

MANAGING EDITOR: Kristi Hart

EDITOR: Pamela Adler

SENIOR PRODUCTION EDITOR: Jennifer Mazurkie

COVER DESIGN: Paul Dinovo

INTERIOR DESIGN: Nick Anderson

MANUFACTURING MANAGER: Kevin Watt

The Betty Crocker Kitchens seal guarantees success in your kitchen. Every recipe has been tested in America's Most Trusted Kitchens™ to meet our high standards of reliability, easy preparation and great taste.

FOR MORE GREAT IDEAS VISIT *BettyCrocker*.com

Dear Friends,

Don't you love the ease of buying a rotisserie chicken? You can make warm, inviting—and surprisingly simple—meals starting with a ready-to-eat rotisserie chicken. This versatile bird can be the star of the meal, when supported by easy appetizers, sides and dessert. Try the easy menus (pages 13 to 38) like the Family Night Dinner menu or the Brunch Is On menu—dinner will play to a full house!

Or maybe you'd like to use a rotisserie chicken as a starting point for recipes—it's a snap. You'll find more than 125 clever recipes for that store-bought rotisserie chicken you just picked up. Enjoy creating delicious dishes such as Mom's Homey Chicken Soup (page 40), Mediterranean Chicken Salad (page 90) or Chicken Divan (page 196)—who would guess they began from a rotisserie chicken?

Check out the **wing it!** tip that accompanies each recipe for helpful information about the ingredients, suggests tasty substitutions or time-saving tactics, or simple additions to make dinner extra special. And if you're short on time, be sure to check out the 🕐 **super express** recipes which can be prepared in just 20 minutes or less. A bird in the hand was never so convenient!

In addition, there's a useful overview of yields, carving tips and storage ideas for your fridge and freezer. The Pantry Planner will help you create a well-stocked kitchen, so when you bring your chicken home, you'll be able to pull together a great dinner, without any fuss or bother. And cleanup is a breeze, since you don't mess up the kitchen roasting a chicken. It's minimum fuss and maximum results for time-crunched home cooks.

Betty Crocker Dinner Made Easy with Rotisserie Chicken turns store-bought chicken into a winning, home-cooked meal.

Warmly,

Betty Crocker

dinner made easy with rotisserie chicken
Contents

All About Rotisserie Chicken

You'll never run out of things to do with a rotisserie chicken. It's so versatile that it earns an "A" for cooperation in the kitchen. The only thing that might ruffle your feathers is trying to decide what flavor of rotisserie chicken to buy. It comes plain, of course, but flavors such as lemon herb, barbecue and garlic can add a touch of pizzazz. The flavor is mainly on the skin, so you can use the meat from any flavored chicken for the recipes in this cookbook.

Use Your Favorites!

Are you partial to certain parts of the chicken, such as breasts or drumsticks? No problem! Use any of your favorite chicken pieces in any of the recipes in this book that call for a cut-up rotisserie chicken.

Handling Rotisserie Chicken Safely

Pick up your rotisserie chicken as the last item on your shopping list. Be sure the chicken is hot when you select it from the heated case. Follow the same food-safety guidelines as for all foods: Keep hot foods hot, which is 140°F or warmer, and always refrigerate the chicken within 2 hours of purchasing (1 hour when the air temperature is above 90°F).

If you are going to use the chicken for a recipe, remove the meat from the bones, cut it up and use it immediately. To use later in a recipe or if you have leftovers, cut the meat from the bones into small pieces, place in a resealable plastic food-storage bag or container with a cover, and refrigerate for use within 4 days. Or place in a freezer container with a cover or a resealable plastic freezer bag and freeze up to 4 months. Thaw frozen cooked chicken in the refrigerator.

How Much Rotisserie Chicken?

The size of rotisserie chickens does vary from store to store. An average weight for a rotisserie chicken is about 2 pounds (32 ounces). You will get the following amount of cut-up meat from a 2-pound chicken:

Whole chicken	3 cups
White meat only	2 cups
Dark meat only	1 cup

Carving Your Rotisserie Chicken

Use a sharp carving knife and a meat fork for best results—safely—when carving. A carving knife works best because it has a long, curved blade. A meat fork has a long handle and two tines. While carving, keep the chicken from moving by holding it in place with a meat fork. Carve on a stable cutting surface, such as a cutting board, meat carving board or platter to catch the juices.

1 Place the chicken, breast up and with its legs to your right if you're right-handed or to the left if left-handed.

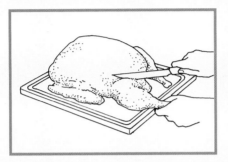

2 While gently pulling the leg and thigh away from the body, cut through the joint between leg and body. Separate the drumstick and thigh by cutting down through the connecting joint.

3 Make a deep horizontal cut into the breast just above the wing joint.

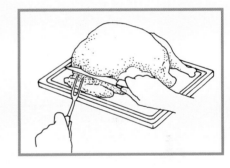

4 Carve thin slices down to the horizontal cut, working from outer edge of breast to the center.

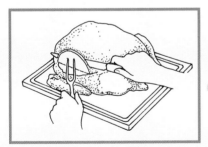

5 While gently pulling the wing away from the body, cut through the joint between wing and body.

6 Repeat steps on the other side of the chicken.

Stocking Your Pantry for Easy and Fast Cooking

Having a wide variety of food and ingredients on hand in your cupboard, refrigerator and freezer offers tremendous flexibility when you are cooking dinner. This pantry list covers all the basics of easy cooking; feel free to add your own favorites to it. If you have a well-stocked pantry, you'll be able to prepare any of the rotisserie chicken recipes in this book even on those days when you don't have time to shop. And even if you don't have all the items stocked, you'll still be able to make great meals from a partially stocked pantry.

Produce

Fruits
- apples, bananas, grapes
- citrus fruits (lemons, oranges)

Vegetables
- carrots
- onions
- potatoes
- coleslaw mix
- salad mix

Bakery

- breads (sandwich bread, rolls, bagels)

Refrigerated Foods

Breads and Dough Products
- pita breads
- prepared doughs (biscuit, breadsticks, pizza crust)
- ready-to-eat garlic or cheese breads
- ready-to-use pizza crust
- refrigerated pasta
- tortillas (corn, flour, flavored)

Condiments

- chopped garlic
- prepared horseradish
- prepared pesto

Dairy
- butter or margarine
- cheese (shredded, sliced)
- cream cheese
- eggs
- milk
- sour cream
- yogurt (plain, flavored)

Frozen Foods

- fruits (blueberries, raspberries, strawberries)
- ice cream and frozen yogurt
- juice concentrate
- ravioli (cheese- or beef-filled)
- vegetables (corn, green beans, favorite combination)

Shelf-Stable Products

Baking Basics

- Bisquick® mix
- chips (semisweet chocolate)
- flour
- nuts (almonds, walnuts, peanuts)

Canned Basics

- beans (kidney, black)
- broth (chicken, vegetable)
- gravy
- green chiles
- mushrooms
- pasta, pizza sauces
- soups
- tomato products (sauce, paste, stewed, diced, seasoned)

Cereals and Snacks

- dry bread crumbs
- cereals
- crackers
- croutons
- taco shells

Condiments and Sauces

- Asian (hoisin, oyster, peanut and sweet-and-sour sauces)
- barbecue sauce
- chutney
- honey
- ice-cream toppings
- ketchup
- maple syrup
- mustards (Dijon, spicy brown, yellow)
- peanut butter
- salsa, picante sauce
- soy sauce, teriyaki sauce

Dressings, Oils and Vinegars

- cooking spray
- oils (vegetable, olive)
- salad dressings
- vinegars (cider, white and red wine)

Herbs, Spices and Dry Mixes

- basil
- bouillon granules or cubes
- chili powder
- cumin
- dry sauce mixes (cheese, gravy, white)
- garlic and onion powder or salt
- herb or seasoning blends, regular or salt-free (Italian seasoning, lemon)
- oregano
- parsley flakes
- pepper seasoning
- tarragon
- thyme

Pasta, Rice, Grains and Potatoes

- couscous
- instant potatoes
- noodle and pasta mixes
- pasta (long, short and tube types)
- potato mixes
- rice (white, brown and quick-cooking)
- rice mixes

Fix It Fast!

Starting with store-bought rotisserie chicken already saves you time in the kitchen, and you can put dinner on the table quickly by choosing from the following recipes. Recipes ready in 20 minutes or less are tagged with 🕐 *super express* throughout the book to make them easy to spot.

15 Minutes or Less 🕐*super express*

20 Minutes 🕐*super express*

25 Minutes

30 Minutes

1 Easy Dinner Menus

Casual Get-Together

Feeling spontaneous tonight? Call a few friends and then pick up a rotisserie chicken on your way home for a quick weeknight gathering. Ask someone to pick up mixed nuts and others to pitch in with their favorite drinks. Good food and great conversation make for a fun-filled evening.

mixed nuts
Toss with soy sauce and enjoy the tasty crunch.

rotisserie chicken

creamy confetti succotash ►

mashed potatoes
No time to mash your own potatoes? Get them from the supermarket deli or refrigerated section.

pound cake sundaes
Top with a scoop of ice cream, a drizzle of chocolate sauce and some sliced strawberries.

Creamy Confetti Succotash

prep: **10 min**
cook: **10 min**

1 tablespoon butter or margarine

1 small red or green bell pepper, chopped (1/2 cup)

2 medium green onions, sliced (2 tablespoons)

1 package (10 ounces) frozen whole kernel corn or 2 cups fresh whole kernel corn

1 cup frozen baby lima beans

1/4 cup half-and-half

2 teaspoons chopped fresh or 1/2 teaspoon dried marjoram leaves

1/4 teaspoon salt

1/8 teaspoon pepper

1 Melt butter in 8-inch skillet over medium-high heat. Cook bell pepper and onions in butter 2 to 3 minutes, stirring occasionally, until crisp-tender.

2 Stir in remaining ingredients; reduce heat to medium-low. Cover and cook 5 to 6 minutes, stirring occasionally, until vegetables are tender.

wing it!

This convenient succotash, made with frozen vegetables, can be made year-round, but in the summer months, it's even more delicious if you use fresh corn cut off the cob. Fresh corn on the cob is at its peak in summer.

Creamy Confetti Succotash

Mexican Fiesta

Say olé! Put on some mariachi music and turn your dinner into a meal with south-of-the-border flair. Use tortilla baskets for fun salsa holders. They're easy! For each basket, invert a 6-ounce custard cup on a cookie sheet, and spray with nonstick cooking spray. Place one 8- to 10-inch flour tortilla over each custard cup. Bake at 400° for 5 to 8 minutes or until crisp. Remove from the custard cups and cool. The best part about these baskets is that you can eat them!

bell pepper nachos
Sprinkle shredded mozzarella or Monterey Jack cheese over slices of green, red and yellow peppers; pop in the microwave to melt the cheese.

rotisserie chicken
Serve with a side of chunky salsa—the hot one if you dare!

slices of tomatoes and avocados
Drizzle with olive oil and sprinkle with salt and pepper.

hot cooked rice
Sprinkle with chopped fresh cilantro.

toasted bananas with ice cream ▶

Toasted Bananas

prep: **10 min**
bake: **8 min**

3 firm, ripe medium bananas

2 tablespoons lemon juice

6 flour tortillas (8 or 10 inches in diameter)

1/4 cup sugar

3/4 teaspoon ground cinnamon

2 tablespoons butter or margarine, melted

1/3 cup chocolate, butterscotch or caramel ice-cream topping

Chocolate or vanilla ice cream, if desired

wing it!

Add some chopped walnuts or pecans with the cinnamon and sugar to give your guests a nutty surprise.

1 Heat oven to 450°. Grease cookie sheet. Peel bananas and cut lengthwise in half; brush with lemon juice. Place 1 banana half on each tortilla. Mix sugar and cinnamon, reserving 1 tablespoon. Sprinkle bananas with sugar-and-cinnamon mixture. Roll each tortilla around banana; place seam side down on cookie sheet. Brush with butter. Sprinkle with reserved sugar-and-cinnamon mixture.

2 Bake 6 to 8 minutes or until golden brown. Place on dessert plates. Drizzle with ice-cream topping. Serve with ice cream.

Toasted Bananas

Enjoy Sunday Supper

Celebrate Sunday! Set the scene for a relaxed meal starting with your favorite flavored rotisserie chicken. Have some fun and have everyone create their own place setting. Cover the table with brown wrapping paper and let everyone design their own place setting with rubber stamps and ink pads. Stamp away!

rotisserie chicken

potato salad
Mustard- or dill-flavored salad from the deli section would make a marvelous side.

mixed vegetables
Drizzle a bag of cooked frozen mixed vegetables with olive oil and a sprinkle of garlic salt.

warm biscuits with honey
Mix up a quick batch of biscuits using Bisquick mix.

triple-berry shortcakes ▶

Triple-Berry Shortcakes

prep: 10 min
stand: 20 min

1 pint (2 cups) strawberries, sliced

1 cup raspberries

1 cup blueberries

1/3 cup sugar

1/4 cup raspberry- or orange-flavored liqueur or orange juice

6 sponge shortcake cups

1 1/2 cups lemon sorbet or sherbet

1 Toss berries, sugar and liqueur. Let stand 20 minutes.

2 Top each shortcake cup with berries and sorbet.

wing it!

Sliced peaches, plums, apricots or nectarines also work well for topping these tempting short-cakes. Then add a scoop of French vanilla ice cream on top.

Triple-Berry Shortcakes

Family Night Dinner

There's no better way to turn mealtime into family time than to create kid-pleasing foods with the help of your junior chefs. These no-nonsense favorites give you plenty of what you really want: more time together!

rotisserie chicken

celery and carrot sticks with hummus
Ready-to-serve hummus can be found in the deli section of most supermarkets.

potato nuggets
A bag of these frozen family favorites goes great with chicken.

tangy coleslaw

pudding
Fix two flavors of instant pudding and let everyone choose their favorite.

Tangy Coleslaw

I bag (16 ounces) coleslaw mix

4 medium green onions, sliced

1/3 cup orange marmalade

1/4 cup rice vinegar or white wine vinegar

I tablespoon sugar

I tablespoon dark sesame oil

I 1/2 teaspoons grated gingerroot or I teaspoon ground ginger

I teaspoon salt

1 Mix coleslaw and onions in large bowl.

2 Shake remaining ingredients in tightly covered container; pour over coleslaw mixture. Toss until coleslaw is evenly coated with dressing.

3 Cover and refrigerate at least 30 minutes to blend flavors.

wing it!

Add a twist to this favorite by stirring in 1 cup canned mandarin orange segments, drained. Sprinkle with 2 table-spoons toasted sliced almonds.

Tangy Coleslaw

The Greeks invented the Olympics—so why not honor them by having everyone remember their greatest sports feat? Just sharing competing stories is fun enough, no need for anyone to expect a medal!

Greek salad ▶

rotisserie chicken
Serve creamy cucumber salad dressing on the side for a quick cucumber-yogurt type sauce.

lemon rice
Stir lemon juice and grated peel into hot cooked rice.

pita bread

rice pudding
The classic Greek dessert, it can be found in the refrigerated section of many supermarkets.

Greek Salad

prep: 15 min

Oregano Vinaigrette (below)

6 cups mixed greens

1 bunch green onions, cut into 1/2-inch pieces

1 medium cucumber, sliced

24 pitted Greek or ripe olives

10 radishes, sliced

1 cup crumbled feta cheese (4 ounces)

1 medium carrot, shredded (3/4 cup)

1 Prepare Oregano Vinaigrette.

2 Toss dressing and remaining ingredients except cheese and carrot. Sprinkle salad with cheese and carrot.

Oregano Vinaigrette

1/2 cup olive oil

1/3 cup wine vinegar

1 tablespoon chopped fresh or 1 teaspoon dried oregano leaves

1/2 teaspoon salt

Shake all ingredients in tightly covered container.

wing it!

To save time, buy shredded carrots in the produce section, or use your favorite bottled vinaigrette dressing.

Greek Salad

Kids like to help in the kitchen, so start them off with putting together the mini carrots and dip. They may also want to help you with the baking—the Caramel-Pecan Brownies are a fun project for everyone.

rotisserie chicken

mini carrots with ranch dressing dip
Dip the mini carrots into small individual bowls of dressing.

mashed potatoes
Make instant mashed potatoes or purchase from the deli or refrigerated section at the supermarket.

Texas toast
Spread butter on both sides of thick-cut bread slices, sprinkle with seasoned salt and broil for 2 to 4 minutes, turning once, until lightly toasted.

caramel-pecan brownies ▶

Caramel-Pecan Brownies

prep: **20 min**
bake: **25 min**

I cup sugar	I/2 teaspoon baking powder
I/2 cup butter or margarine, softened	I/4 teaspoon salt
I teaspoon vanilla	I/2 cup chopped walnuts, if desired
2 eggs	I/2 cup coarsely chopped pecans
2/3 cup all-purpose flour	I2 vanilla caramels
I/2 cup baking cocoa	I tablespoon milk

1 Heat oven to 350°. Grease square pan, 9 × 9 × 2 inches.

2 Beat sugar, butter, vanilla and eggs in large bowl with electric mixer on medium speed, or mix with spoon. Stir remaining ingredients except walnuts. Stir in walnuts.

3 Spread batter evenly in pan. Sprinkle pecans over the batter. Bake 20 to 25 minutes or until toothpick inserted in center comes out clean. Heat vanilla caramels and milk over low heat, and stir until everything is melted and smooth. Drizzle caramel over warm brownies. Cool completely. Cut into 4 rows by 4 rows.

wing it!

Pop a pan of brownie mix in the oven or make these tasty tidbits and let them bake while you enjoy lunch.

Caramel-Pecan Brownies

Experience some of the delicious culinary heritage of China with this delectable dinner. End the trip by dipping purchased fortune cookies in melted chocolate. Then check out your luck by reading the fortune tucked inside.

spring rolls
Buy the bite-size ones that are readily available in the frozen food section of most supermarkets.

rotisserie chicken
Serve duck sauce or sweet-and-sour sauce in individual bowls for dipping. You can find them in the condiments or Asian foods section of your supermarket.

stir-fried green beans and peppers

hot cooked white rice
Sprinkle with toasted sesame seeds.

lemon sorbet

Stir-Fried Green Beans and Peppers

prep: **10 min**
cook: **8 min**

1/2 pound green beans, cut crosswise in half

1 medium yellow or red bell pepper, cut into 1/2-inch pieces

1 tablespoon vegetable oil

2 teaspoons chopped fresh or 1/2 teaspoon dried marjoram leaves

wing it!

In a festive mood? Use 1 small yellow and 1 small red bell pepper, cut into 1/2-inch pieces, for extra color.

1 Heat 1/4 cup of water and beans to boiling in a 10-inch skillet over high heat. Reduce heat. Cover and simmer about 5 minutes or until beans are tender; drain any remaining liquid. (It's important to drain off any remaining water from the skillet after cooking the beans to keep the stir-fry crisp. For ease, pour beans into a strainer or colander and then return them to the skillet.)

2 Add bell pepper and oil to the beans in the skillet. Increase heat to medium-high. Stir-fry about 2 minutes, until bell pepper is crisp-tender. Stir in marjoram.

Stir-Fried Green Beans and Peppers

Make It Italian Tonight

Everybody loves Italian! Gather the family for this easy menu of traditional foods and flavors. Decorate your table with white, red and green candles—the colors of the Italian flag. Top the evening off with a scoop of spumoni ice cream.

assorted olives

rotisserie chicken

sliced fresh tomatoes and mozzarella cheese

Drizzle with olive oil and sprinkle with chopped fresh basil.

asparagus with parmesan ▶

pasta Alfredo

Toss your favorite hot cooked pasta with a jar of Alfredo sauce.

garlic bread

Save time by picking up a loaf from the bakery or frozen food section of your supermarket.

Asparagus with Parmesan

prep: 5 min
cook: 4 min
bake: 10 min

1 1/2 pounds asparagus

1 tablespoon olive oil

1 tablespoon butter or margarine

1 medium green onion, chopped
(1 tablespoon)

1 clove garlic, finely chopped

1/2 teaspoon salt

1/4 teaspoon freshly ground pepper

1/4 cup shredded Parmesan cheese

wing it!

Use frozen asparagus when fresh asparagus is not available. Cook two 10-ounce packages of frozen asparagus spears according to package directions.

1 Heat 1 inch salted water (1/2 teaspoon to 1 cup water) to boiling in 3-quart saucepan. Add asparagus. Heat to boiling; reduce heat. Simmer uncovered 4 minutes; drain.

2 Meanwhile, heat oven to 375°. Place oil, butter, onion and garlic in ungreased square pan, 8 × 8 × 2 inches. Heat uncovered in oven 5 minutes.

3 Spread asparagus in pan. Sprinkle with salt, pepper and cheese. Bake uncovered about 10 minutes or until cheese is melted.

Asparagus with Parmesan

Make dinner special with your sweetie. Set the scene for an evening of relaxation and romance. Play your favorite music, relax and light some candles. Bon appétit!

Mediterranean salad
Toss a couple cups of mixed salad greens with a jar of undrained marinated artichoke hearts. Sprinkle with crumbled feta cheese and top with some pitted marinated olives.

rotisserie chicken

couscous
Stir some dried cranberries or golden raisins and a sliced green onion into warm couscous. Sprinkle with toasted slivered almonds.

balsamic vegetables
Toss a box of cooked frozen vegetables with 1/3 cup of balsamic dressing.

white chocolate–dipped strawberries
Let the chocolate coating set while you enjoy this meal.

White Chocolate–Dipped Strawberries

prep: **10 min**
refrigerate: **30 min**

9 to 12 large strawberries with leaves

1/2 bag (6 ounces) white baking chips (1 cup)

1 1/2 teaspoons shortening

1/4 cup semisweet chocolate chips

1/2 teaspoon shortening

1 Cover a cookie sheet with waxed paper.

2 Rinse strawberries with cool water, and pat dry with paper towels.

3 Heat white baking chips and 1 1/2 teaspoons shortening in a saucepan over low heat, stirring constantly, until chips are melted.

4 Dip each strawberry three-fourths of the way into melted white chips, leaving the top of the strawberry and leaves uncoated. Place dipped strawberries on waxed paper–covered cookie sheet.

5 Heat semisweet chocolate chips and 1/2 teaspoon shortening in another small saucepan over low heat, stirring constantly, until chocolate chips are melted.

6 Drizzle melted chocolate chips over dipped strawberries, using a small spoon. Refrigerate uncovered about 30 minutes or until coating is set.

wing it!

Save time by placing chocolate chips and shortening in a small microwavable bowl. Microwave uncovered on Medium 1 minute; stir. Microwave 2 to 3 minutes longer, until mixture can be stirred smooth.

White Chocolate–Dipped Strawberries

For fun, place disposable cameras on the table and turn dinner into a vacation photo "op." Don't have a set of steel drums? Don't worry, be happy and crank up the sounds of your favorite Caribbean musicians.

rotisserie chicken

coconut rice
Substitute coconut milk for half the liquid when making white rice.

fruit salad
Toss cut-up fresh fruit such as mango, papaya and melons with honey, lime juice and slivered almonds.

green beans
Toss with toasted sesame seeds and olive oil.

chocolate-laced kiwi with orange sauce ▶

Chocolate-Laced Kiwi
with Orange Sauce

prep: 15 min

1/2 cup plain yogurt

1 tablespoon frozen (partially thawed) orange juice concentrate

4 large kiwifruit, peeled and cut into 1/4-inch slices

2 tablespoons semisweet chocolate chips

1 teaspoon shortening

1 Mix yogurt and orange juice concentrate; spoon 2 tablespoons onto each of 4 dessert plates. Arrange kiwifruit on yogurt mixture.

2 Melt chocolate chips and shortening over low heat, stirring constantly. Carefully drizzle chocolate in thin lines over kiwifruit.

wing it!

If you don't have kiwifruit, use whatever fresh fruit you have on hand, such as banana or strawberry slices.

Chocolate-Laced Kiwi with Orange Sauce

Head Down South

SERVES 6

Head south for this down-home mouthwatering feast that's sure to please. Get high praise with low-country cooking. Sit back, relax and enjoy the slow southern rhythms of the meal. Or liven things up with some Dixieland music.

lemonade or iced tea
Serve with slices of orange and lemon for an extra fruity twist.

rotisserie chicken
Barbecue is the best choice for a fantistic down-south dinner.

mashed sweet potatoes
Add a tablespoon of brown sugar and butter to a can of heated sweet potatoes or yams.

hot and spicy collard greens ▶

pecan pie

Hot and Spicy Collard Greens

prep: 10 min
cook: 10 min

2 tablespoons butter or margarine

2 tablespoons finely chopped onions

1 to 2 teaspoons grated gingerroot

2 pounds collard greens, coarsely chopped

1 serrano chili, seeded and finely chopped

1 Melt butter in Dutch oven over medium heat.

2 Add remaining ingredients. Cook, stirring frequently, about 10 minutes or until onion and greens are tender; drain.

wing it!

Can't find collard greens? Use fresh spinach or mustard greens instead.

Hot and Spicy Collard Greens

The weekend's a perfect time to gather friends and loved ones for an easy brunch. Create seasonal centerpieces by collecting leaves in autumn to sprinkle on the table, or daisies in summer to brighten up the room.

café au lait
Mix equal parts of hot coffee and hot milk.

rotisserie chicken
Add some zest by buying the lemon-pepper flavor.

Italian new potato salad ▶

melon platter
Arrange slices of cantaloupe and honey melon—or any melons that are in season—on a platter. Tuck in some clusters of green or red grapes and a few fresh mint springs if you have them.

raspberry–white chocolate muffins ▶

Italian New Potato Salad

prep: 15 min
cook: 12 min

3/4 pound green beans

**1 1/2 pounds new potatoes
(10 to 12 small), cut into fourths**

1/4 cup water

**1/2 cup Italian dressing or balsamic
vinaigrette**

1/4 cup chopped red onion

**1 can (2 1/4 ounces) sliced ripe olives,
drained**

wing it!

If you don't have new potatoes on hand, use 5 medium potatoes cut into about 3/4-inch cubes.

1 Cut beans in half if desired. Place beans, potatoes and water in 2-quart microwavable casserole. Cover and microwave on High 10 to 12 minutes, rotating dish 1/2 turn every 4 minutes, until potatoes are tender; drain.

2 Place beans and potatoes in large glass or plastic bowl. Pour dressing over vegetables; toss. Add onion and olives; toss.

Italian New Potato Salad

prep: **10 min**
bake: **18 min**

Raspberry–White Chocolate Muffins

2 cups Original Bisquick mix

1/2 cup white baking chips

1/3 cup sugar

2/3 cup milk

2 tablespoons vegetable oil

1 egg

1 cup raspberries

1 Heat oven to 400°. Grease bottoms only of 12 medium muffin cups, 2 1/2 × 1 1/4 inches or line with paper baking cups.

2 Stir all ingredients except raspberries in large bowl just until moistened. Fold in raspberries. Divide batter evenly among cups.

3 Bake 15 to 18 minutes or until golden brown. Cool slightly; remove from pan to wire rack.

Raspberry–White Chocolate Muffins

2 Super Soups, Stews and Chilies

Mom's Homey Chicken Soup

prep: 20 min
cook: 30 min

wing it!

Who wouldn't welcome a steamy bowl of old-fashioned chicken noodle soup on a cold day? One taste and it will be a family favorite.

3 cups homemade or canned ready-to-serve chicken broth	2 tablespoons chicken bouillon granules
3 cups water	1 tablespoon chopped fresh parsley
1 cup baby-cut carrots	1 tablespoon chopped fresh or 1 teaspoon dried thyme leaves
2 medium stalks celery, sliced (1 cup)	1 cup frozen egg noodles (from 12-ounce bag)
1 medium onion, chopped (1/2 cup)	2 cups cut-up cooked chicken
2 cloves garlic, finely chopped	

1 Heat all ingredients except noodles and chicken to boiling in 4-quart Dutch oven.

2 Stir in noodles; reduce heat. Simmer uncovered 20 to 25 minutes, adding chicken for last 5 minutes, until vegetables and noodles are tender.

1 SERVING: Calories 160 (Calories from Fat 45); Fat 5g (Saturated 1g); Cholesterol 45mg; Sodium 1850mg; Carbohydrate 11g (Dietary Fiber 2g); Protein 18g • **% DAILY VALUE:** Vitamin A 80%; Vitamin C 4%; Calcium 4%; Iron 8% • **DIET EXCHANGES:** 1/2 Starch, 1 Vegetable, 2 Lean Meat • **CARBOHYDRATE CHOICES:** 1

Asian Chicken Noodle Soup

prep: 15 min
cook: 8 min

3 cups water

1 package (3 ounces) chicken-flavor ramen noodle soup mix

2 cups cut-up cooked chicken

2 medium stalks bok choy (with leaves), cut into 1/4-inch slices

1 medium carrot, sliced (1/2 cup)

1 teaspoon sesame oil, if desired

1 Heat water to boiling in 3-quart saucepan. Break block of noodles (reserve seasoning packet). Stir noodles, chicken, bok choy and carrot into water. Heat to boiling; reduce heat. Simmer uncovered 3 minutes, stirring occasionally.

2 Stir in contents of seasoning packet and sesame oil.

wing it!

The reason for breaking the block of dry noodles into pieces is that, if you don't, it will stay in one large piece as it cooks. The soup will also be easier to eat because the broken noodles won't be so long and unwieldy.

1 SERVING: Calories 230 (Calories from Fat 80); Fat 9g (Saturated 3g); Cholesterol 60mg; Sodium 440mg; Carbohydrate 15g (Dietary Fiber 1g); Protein 22g • % DAILY VALUE: Vitamin A 82%; Vitamin C 14%; Calcium 6%; Iron 10% • DIET EXCHANGES: 1 Starch, 2 1/2 Lean Meat, 1/2 Fat • CARBOHYDRATE CHOICES: 1

Chicken Noodle Soup

1 tablespoon olive or vegetable oil

2 cloves garlic, finely chopped

8 medium green onions, sliced (4 tablespoons)

2 medium carrots, chopped (1 cup)

2 cups cubed cooked chicken

2 cups uncooked egg noodles (4 ounces)

1 tablespoon chopped fresh parsley or 1 teaspoon parsley flakes

1/4 teaspoon pepper

1 dried bay leaf

3 cans (14 1/2 ounces each) ready-to-serve chicken broth

1 Heat oil in 3-quart saucepan over medium heat. Cook garlic, onions and carrots in oil 4 minutes, stirring occasionally.

2 Stir in remaining ingredients. Heat to boiling; reduce heat. Cover and simmer about 10 minutes, stirring occasionally, until carrots and noodles are tender. Remove bay leaf.

prep: 15 min
cook: 15 min

wing it!

Although available fresh, most bay leaves sold in the United States are dried. Slightly bitter in flavor, this aromatic herb comes from the evergreen bay laurel tree, which is native to the Mediterranean area. Bay leaves are always removed from the food before serving.

1 SERVING: Calories 320 (Calories from Fat 100); Fat 11g (Saturated 3g); Cholesterol 85mg; Sodium 1390mg; Carbohydrate 25g (Dietary Fiber 2g); Protein 30g • % DAILY VALUE: Vitamin A 100%; Vitamin C 8%; Calcium 6%; Iron 8% • DIET EXCHANGES: 1 Starch, 2 Vegetable, 3 Lean Meat, 1 Fat • CARBOHYDRATE CHOICES: 1 1/2

Chicken Noodle Soup

Chicken and Root Vegetable Soup

prep: 20 min
cook: 30 min

wing it!

Parsnips are cousins to carrots, celery and parsley. They look like large white carrots and, like carrots, should be peeled. They are a favorite in Europe, prized for their sweetness and versatility. Peak season is October through April.

2 tablespoons butter or margarine

1 small onion, finely chopped (1/4 cup)

2 medium carrots, thinly sliced (1 cup)

3 medium parsnips, peeled and sliced (1 cup)

1 medium leek, sliced (2 cups)

7 cups ready-to-serve chicken broth

1 cup uncooked orzo or rosamarina pasta (6 ounces)

2 cups shredded cooked chicken

2 tablespoons chopped fresh or 2 teaspoons dried dill weed

1/2 teaspoon salt

1 Melt butter in Dutch oven over medium heat. Cook onion, carrots, parsnips and leek in butter about 5 minutes, stirring occasionally, until carrots are tender.

2 Stir in broth and pasta. Heat to boiling; reduce heat to low. Cover and simmer about 15 minutes, stirring occasionally, until pasta is tender.

3 Stir in remaining ingredients. Cover and simmer about 5 minutes or until hot.

1 SERVING: Calories 320 (Calories from Fat 90); Fat 10g (Saturated 2g); Cholesterol 40mg; Sodium 1600mg; Carbohydrate 39g (Dietary Fiber 5g); Protein 24g • % DAILY VALUE: Vitamin A 60%; Vitamin C 12%; Calcium 8%; Iron 18% • DIET EXCHANGES: 2 Starch, 2 Vegetable, 2 Lean Meat • CARBOHYDRATE CHOICES: 2 1/2

Chicken and Root Vegetable Soup

prep: 10 min
cook: 25 min

wing it!

Nothing tops off this soup better than these two-ingredient dumplings! Stir 1 teaspoon of a favorite dried herb into the dough for extra flavor.

Chicken-Vegetable Soup with Mini-Dumplings

2 cups cut-up cooked chicken

4 cups ready-to-serve chicken broth

1 tablespoon chopped fresh parsley

1 tablespoon chopped fresh thyme leaves

2 cloves garlic, finely chopped

1 bag (1 pound) frozen mixed vegetables or soup vegetables, thawed and drained

1 cup Original Bisquick mix

1/3 cup milk

1 Heat all ingredients except Bisquick mix and milk to boiling in 3-quart saucepan.

2 Stir Bisquick mix and milk until soft dough forms. Drop dough by teaspoonfuls onto boiling soup. If dumplings sink into soup, carefully bring them to top of broth using slotted spoon. Reduce heat to low.

3 Cook uncovered 10 minutes. Cover and cook 10 minutes longer.

1 SERVING: Calories 235 (Calories from Fat 65); Fat 7g (Saturated 2g); Cholesterol 40mg; Sodium 1030mg; Carbohydrate 23g (Dietary Fiber 4g); Protein 20g • % DAILY VALUE: Vitamin A 66%; Vitamin C 2%; Calcium 8%; Iron 2% • DIET EXCHANGES: 1 Starch, 3 Vegetable, 2 Lean Meat • CARBOHYDRATE CHOICES: 1 1/2

Chunky Chicken Soup with Pasta Shells

prep: 25 min
cook: 30 min

1 tablespoon olive or vegetable oil

2 medium onions, chopped (1 cup)

1 medium green bell pepper, chopped (1 cup)

2 medium carrots, chopped (1 cup)

2 cloves garlic, finely chopped

2 cans (14 1/2 ounces each) ready-to-serve chicken broth

1 can (14 1/2 ounces) diced tomatoes, undrained

1 can (15 to 16 ounces) kidney beans, rinsed and drained

1 cup diced cooked chicken

2 teaspoons chopped fresh or 1/2 teaspoon dried basil leaves

1/2 cup uncooked small pasta shells (2 ounces)

1/4 cup shredded Parmesan cheese

1 Heat oil in Dutch oven over medium-high heat. Cook onions, bell pepper, carrots and garlic in oil 2 to 3 minutes, stirring frequently, until vegetables are crisp-tender.

2 Stir in broth, tomatoes, beans, chicken and basil. Heat to boiling; reduce heat to medium-low. Cook 10 minutes, stirring occasionally.

3 Stir in pasta. Cook 10 to 12 minutes, stirring occasionally, until pasta is tender. Top each serving with cheese.

wing it!

Great for a quick hearty meal, this soup is perfect anytime served with soft breadsticks or a loaf of ficelle, which is a long and thin version of French bread.

1 SERVING: Calories 380 (Calories from Fat 90); Fat 10g (Saturated 3g); Cholesterol 35mg; Sodium 1500mg; Carbohydrate 54g (Dietary Fiber 11g); Protein 30g • % DAILY VALUE: Vitamin A 100%; Vitamin C 40%; Calcium 18%; Iron 28% • DIET EXCHANGES: 3 Starch, 3 Vegetable, 2 Lean Meat • CARBOHYDRATE CHOICES: 3 1/2

Lemony Chicken-Lentil Soup

prep: 15 min
cook: 55 min

wing it!

You'll really like this fresh lemony lentil soup. For a fun color change, use pink lentils.

1 tablespoon olive or vegetable oil

1 medium onion, chopped (1/2 cup)

3 medium carrots, chopped (1 1/2 cups)

2 cloves garlic, finely chopped

1 cup dried lentils (8 ounces), sorted and rinsed

2 tablespoons tomato paste

2 cans (14 1/2 ounces each) ready-to-serve chicken broth

2 cups cut-up cooked chicken

2 tablespoons grated lemon peel

1 Heat oil in 3-quart saucepan over medium-high heat. Cook onion, carrots and garlic in oil about 5 minutes, stirring occasionally, until carrots are tender.

2 Stir in lentils, tomato paste and broth. Heat to boiling; reduce heat to low. Cover and simmer about 40 minutes or until lentils are tender.

3 Stir in chicken and lemon peel. Cook about 5 minutes or until hot.

1 SERVING: Calories 225 (Calories from Fat 65); Fat 7g (Saturated 1g); Cholesterol 40mg; Sodium 680mg; Carbohydrate 24g (Dietary Fiber 8g); Protein 24g • % DAILY VALUE: Vitamin A 78%; Vitamin C 8%; Calcium 4%; Iron 24% • DIET EXCHANGES: 1 Starch, 2 Vegetable, 2 Lean Meat • CARBOHYDRATE CHOICES: 1 1/2

Lemony Chicken-Lentil Soup

Rio Grande Chicken Soup

prep: 10 min
cook: 15 min

wing it!

Change the flavor profile of this soup by varying the salsa. Use hot salsa if you love the heat, medium if you like a little heat or mild if you don't want any heat.

I can (14 1/2 ounces) ready-to-serve chicken broth

I can (28 ounces) whole tomatoes, undrained

I jar (16 ounces) thick 'n chunky salsa (2 cups)

2 to 3 teaspoons chili powder

1/2 bag (1-pound size) frozen corn, broccoli and red peppers (or other combination)

I cup uncooked cavatappi pasta (3 ounces)

2 cups cut-up cooked chicken

1/4 cup chopped fresh parsley

1 Heat broth, tomatoes, salsa and chili powder to boiling in 4-quart Dutch oven, breaking up tomatoes. Stir in frozen vegetables and pasta. Heat to boiling; reduce heat.

2 Simmer uncovered about 12 minutes, stirring occasionally, until pasta and vegetables are tender. Stir in chicken and parsley; cook until hot.

1 SERVING: Calories 225 (Calories from Fat 45); Fat 5g (Saturated 1g); Cholesterol 40mg; Sodium 960mg; Carbohydrate 25g (Dietary Fiber 4g); Protein 20g • **% DAILY VALUE:** Vitamin A 36%; Vitamin C 34%; Calcium 8%; Iron 18% • **DIET EXCHANGES:** 1 Starch, 2 Vegetable, 2 Lean Meat • **CARBOHYDRATE CHOICES:** 1 1/2

Spring Arborio Rice and Chicken Soup

prep: 20 min
cook: 30 min

2 tablespoons olive or vegetable oil

1 small onion, finely chopped (1/4 cup)

1 cup cubed cooked chicken

1 cup uncooked Arborio or other short-grain rice

6 cups ready-to-serve chicken broth

1/4 cup chopped fresh mint leaves

3 tablespoons chopped fresh parsley

1 package (10 ounces) frozen green peas

Freshly grated Parmesan cheese

1 Heat oil in Dutch oven over medium heat. Cook onion in oil, stirring frequently for about 5 minutes, or until onion is translucent.

2 Stir in chicken and rice. Cook 1 minute over medium heat, stirring frequently, until rice begins to brown. Pour 1/2 cup of the broth over rice mixture. Cook uncovered, stirring frequently, until broth is absorbed. Continue cooking 15 to 20 minutes, adding broth 1/2 cup at a time and stirring frequently, until rice is creamy and almost tender and 3 cups broth have been used.

3 Stir in remaining 3 cups broth, the mint, parsley and frozen peas. Cook over medium heat about 5 minutes or until hot. Serve with cheese.

wing it!

Arborio is an Italian-grown rice and its high starch content gives risotto its creamy texture. Like pasta, it is cooked until al dente, meaning "to the tooth" so it isn't over-cooked and soft.

1 **SERVING:** Calories 280 (Calories from Fat 70); Fat 8g (Saturated 1g); Cholesterol 35mg; Sodium 1130mg; Carbohydrate 36g (Dietary Fiber 3g); Protein 19g • % **DAILY VALUE:** Vitamin A 8%; Vitamin C 6%; Calcium 6%; Iron 16% • **DIET EXCHANGES:** 2 Starch, 1 Vegetable, 2 Lean Meat • **CARBOHYDRATE CHOICES:** 2 1/2

Summertime Chicken Gazpacho

prep: 30 min
chill: 1 hr

wing it!

Traditionally, gazpacho uses fresh bread crumbs to add body to the soup. This version does, too. Plus the spicy eight-vegetable juice adds both flavor and convenience. How much better could it get?

3 slices white bread, crusts removed

3 cloves garlic

2 tablespoons lemon juice

10 medium unpeeled tomatoes, diced (7 1/2 cups)

6 medium green onions, finely chopped (6 tablespoons)

2 medium cucumbers, peeled and diced (2 cups)

2 medium red bell peppers, diced (2 cups)

1 can (46 ounces) spicy eight-vegetable juice

2 tablespoons balsamic vinegar

1/2 teaspoon salt

1 cup cubed cooked chicken

Croutons, if desired

1 Place bread, garlic and lemon juice in a food processor or blender. Cover and process until bread forms fine crumbs.

2 Place bread crumb mixture in large bowl. Stir in remaining ingredients except chicken and croutons. Place half of the bread crumbs and vegetable mixture (about 7 cups) in food processor or blender. Cover and process until smooth. Repeat in small batches if necessary.

3 Stir smooth vegetable mixture into vegetable mixture remaining in bowl. Stir in chicken. Cover and refrigerate at least 1 hour until chilled. Serve with croutons.

1 SERVING: Calories 145 (Calories from Fat 20); Fat 2g (Saturated 0g); Cholesterol 15mg; Sodium 660mg; Carbohydrate 23g (Dietary Fiber 4g); Protein 9g • % DAILY VALUE: Vitamin A 54%; Vitamin C 100%; Calcium 6%; Iron 12% • DIET EXCHANGES: 5 Vegetable • CARBOHYDRATE CHOICES: 1 1/2

Summertime Chicken Gazpacho

Tuscan Tomato Soup

prep: 30 min
cook: 30 min

wingit!

**To save time in
your busy sched-
ule, use your food
processor to
chop the onion,
carrots, basil and
tomatoes.**

2 tablespoons butter or margarine	**2 tablespoons sugar**
1 medium onion, finely chopped (1/2 cup)	**1 teaspoon salt**
2 medium carrots, finely chopped (1/2 cup)	**10 large tomatoes, peeled and coarsely chopped (10 cups)**
1 cup shredded cooked chicken	**1 can (8 ounces) tomato sauce**
1/4 cup chopped fresh basil leaves	**Sliced fresh basil leaves, if desired**

1 Melt butter in Dutch oven over medium-high heat. Cook onion and carrots in butter about 5 minutes, stirring occasionally, until carrot is tender.

2 Stir in chicken, 1/4 cup basil, the sugar, salt, tomatoes and tomato sauce. Heat to boiling; reduce heat to low. Simmer uncovered 20 to 25 minutes, stirring occasionally, until flavors are blended. Serve topped with basil.

1 SERVING: Calories 270 (Calories from Fat 90); Fat 10g (Saturated 2g); Cholesterol 30mg; Sodium 1080mg; Carbohydrate 37g (Dietary Fiber 7g); Protein 15g • **% DAILY VALUE:** Vitamin A 100%; Vitamin C 80%; Calcium 6%; Iron 18% • **DIET EXCHANGES:** 7 Vegetable, 2 Fat • **CARBOHYDRATE CHOICES:** 2 1/2

Tuscan Tomato Soup

Chicken Cordon Bleu Chowder

prep: 15 min
cook: 7 min

wing it!

Chicken or veal cordon bleu is a traditional dish that combines Swiss cheese and ham rolled up in chicken breasts or veal. We have used this flavorful combination in a hearty chowder.

2 cans (19 ounces each) ready-to-serve creamy potato with garlic soup

1 cup cubed cooked chicken

1 cup diced fully cooked ham

1 cup shredded Swiss cheese (4 ounces)

1 tablespoon chopped fresh chives

1. Heat soup, chicken and ham in 3-quart saucepan over medium-high heat 5 minutes, stirring occasionally.

2. Slowly stir in cheese. Cook about 2 minutes, stirring frequently, until cheese is melted. Serve topped with chives.

1 SERVING: Calories 440 (Calories from Fat 260); Fat 29g (Saturated 10g); Cholesterol 90mg; Sodium 1530mg; Carbohydrate 19g (Dietary Fiber 1g); Protein 31g • % DAILY VALUE: Vitamin A 8%; Vitamin C 4%; Calcium 30%; Iron 8% • DIET EXCHANGES: 1 Starch, 1 Vegetable, 4 Lean Meat, 3 Fat • CARBOHYDRATE CHOICES: 1

Chicken Cordon Bleu Chowder

Buffalo Chicken Chili

prep: 20 min
cook: 30 min

wing it!

Buffalo chicken wings are spicy, deep-fried chicken wings that are served with blue cheese dressing and celery sticks. Those great flavors are the basis for this terrific chili topped with crumbled blue cheese and celery.

I tablespoon vegetable oil

I large onion, chopped (I cup)

I medium red or yellow bell pepper, chopped (I cup)

2 cups cubed cooked chicken

I cup ready-to-serve chicken broth

I tablespoon chili powder

5 to 6 drops red pepper sauce

2 cans (15 to 16 ounces each) pinto beans, drained

I can (28 ounces) crushed tomatoes, undrained

I can (15 ounces) tomato sauce with tomato bits

1/4 cup sliced celery

1/4 cup crumbled blue cheese

1 Heat oil in 3-quart saucepan over medium-high heat. Cook onion and bell pepper in oil about 5 minutes, stirring occasionally, until crisp-tender.

2 Stir in remaining ingredients except celery and blue cheese. Heat to boiling; reduce heat to medium-low. Simmer uncovered 10 to 15 minutes, stirring occasionally. Serve topped with celery and blue cheese.

1 SERVING: Calories 480 (Calories from Fat 115); Fat 13g (Saturated 4g); Cholesterol 65mg; Sodium 1700mg; Carbohydrate 70g (Dietary Fiber 21g); Protein 41g • % DAILY VALUE: Vitamin A 78%; Vitamin C 84%; Calcium 24%; Iron 46% • DIET EXCHANGES: 3 Starch, 5 Vegetable, 2 Lean Meat • CARBOHYDRATE CHOICES: 4 1/2

Buffalo Chicken Chili

White Bean Chili

prep: 15 min
cook: 20 min

wing it!

Ground red chilies are made from finely ground dried red chilies and containing no other ingredients. Chili powder starts with ground red chilies but also has cumin and oregano, and it may include paprika, coriander and salt.

1/4 cup butter or margarine

1 large onion, chopped (1 cup)

1 clove garlic, finely chopped

4 cups 1/2-inch cubes cooked chicken

3 cups ready-to-serve chicken broth

2 tablespoons chopped fresh cilantro

1 tablespoon dried basil leaves

2 teaspoons ground red chilies or chili powder

1/4 teaspoon ground cloves

2 cans (15 to 16 ounces each) great northern beans, undrained

1 medium tomato, chopped (3/4 cup)

Blue or yellow corn tortilla chips

1 Melt butter in Dutch oven over medium heat. Cook onion and garlic in butter about 5 minutes, stirring occasionally, until onion is tender.

2 Stir in remaining ingredients except tomato and tortilla chips. Heat to boiling; reduce heat. Cover and simmer 15 minutes, stirring occasionally. Serve with tomato and tortilla chips.

1 SERVING: Calories 415 (Calories from Fat 160); Fat 18g (Saturated 4g); Cholesterol 80mg; Sodium 760mg; Carbohydrate 46g (Dietary Fiber 10g); Protein 43g • % DAILY VALUE: Vitamin A 18%; Vitamin C 4%; Calcium 16%; Iron 40% • DIET EXCHANGES: 3 Starch, 4 Lean Meat, 1/2 Fat • CARBOHYDRATE CHOICES: 3

3 Speedy Salads

 = **super express** ready in 20 minutes or less

prep: 10 min

wingit!

Classic chicken salad can be used as a sandwich filling, to stuff a tomato or to top a wedge of fresh melon. It's even wonderful all by itself served on a lettuce-lined plate with some cut-up fresh vegetables or fruits.

2 SERVINGS

Chicken Salad

1/2 cup mayonnaise or salad dressing

1/4 teaspoon salt

1/4 teaspoon pepper

1 1/2 cups chopped cooked chicken

1 medium stalk celery, chopped (1/2 cup)

1 small onion, finely chopped (1/4 cup)

1 Mix mayonnaise, salt and pepper in medium bowl.

2 Add remaining ingredients. Toss evenly to coat.

1 SERVING: Calories 600 (Calories from Fat 460); Fat 51g (Saturated 9g); Cholesterol 125mg; Sodium 710mg; Carbohydrate 5g (Dietary Fiber 1g); Protein 30g • **% DAILY VALUE:** Vitamin A 2%; Vitamin C 6%; Calcium 4%; Iron 10% • **DIET EXCHANGES:** 1 Vegetable, 4 Medium-Fat Meat, 6 Fat • **CARBOHYDRATE CHOICES:** 0

Chicken Salad with Fruit

prep: 20 min
chill: 2 hr

3 cups cut-up cooked chicken

3/4 cup sliced green grapes

2 medium stalks celery, sliced (1 cup)

2 medium green onions, thinly sliced (2 tablespoons)

1 can (11 ounces) mandarin orange segments, drained

1 can (8 ounces) sliced water chestnuts, drained

1 cup peach or lemon low-fat yogurt

2 tablespoons reduced-sodium soy sauce

Mixed salad greens

1 Mix chicken, grapes, celery, onions, orange segments and water chestnuts in large glass or plastic bowl.

2 Mix yogurt and soy sauce. Pour over chicken mixture; toss. Cover and refrigerate at least 2 hours to blend flavors. Serve on salad greens.

wing it!

Fill up on fiber by serving this salad with slices of crusty whole wheat bread.

1 SERVING: Calories 215 (Calories from Fat 45); Fat 5g (Saturated 2g); Cholesterol 60mg; Sodium 270mg; Carbohydrate 21g (Dietary Fiber 2g); Protein 22g • % DAILY VALUE: Vitamin A 6%; Vitamin C 30%; Calcium 8%; Iron 8% • DIET EXCHANGES: 1 Fruit, 1 Vegetable, 2 1/2 Lean Meat • CARBOHYDRATE CHOICES: 1 1/2

prep: **20 min**

wing it!

If fresh berries aren't at their peak, frozen unsweetened loose-pack raspberries and strawberries can be substituted for the fresh raspberries and strawberries.

4 SERVINGS

Chicken and Berries Salad

Fruity Yogurt Dressing (below)

4 cups bite-size pieces mixed salad greens (iceberg, Bibb, romaine or spinach)

2 cups cut-up cooked chicken

I cup raspberries

1/2 cup sliced strawberries

1/4 cup thinly sliced leek

1/4 cup sliced almonds, toasted

Freshly ground pepper

1 Make Fruity Yogurt Dressing.

2 Toss salad greens, chicken, berries and leek. Sprinkle with almonds.

3 Serve with dressing and pepper.

Fruity Yogurt Dressing

I cup plain nonfat yogurt

1/4 cup raspberries

1/4 cup sliced strawberries

I tablespoon raspberry or red wine vinegar

2 teaspoons sugar

Place all ingredients in blender or food processor. Cover and blend on high speed about 15 seconds or until smooth.

1 SERVING: Calories 255 (Calories from Fat 80); Fat 9g (Saturated 2g); Cholesterol 60mg; Sodium 120mg; Carbohydrate 17g (Dietary Fiber 5g); Protein 26g • % DAILY VALUE: Vitamin A 36%; Vitamin C 64%; Calcium 18%; Iron 12% • DIET EXCHANGES: 1/2 Fruit, 2 Vegetable, 3 Lean Meat • CARBOHYDRATE CHOICES: 1

Chicken and Berries Salad

prep: 10 min

wing it!

Although any assortment of greens will taste great in this salad, the slightly bitter tang of an Italian-style mix with romaine and radicchio is especially nice with the chicken, dried fruit and subtly sweet French dressing.

6 SERVINGS

Chicken and Fruit Tossed Salad

1 bag (10 ounces) salad mix

2 1/2 cups cubed cooked chicken

1 package (6 ounces) diced dried fruits and raisins (about 1 1/4 cups)

1 medium stalk celery, sliced (1/2 cup)

1/2 cup fat-free sweet-spicy French dressing

1 Place salad mix, chicken, dried fruits and celery in large bowl.

2 Pour dressing over mixture; toss lightly to coat.

1 SERVING: Calories 230 (Calories from Fat 35); Fat 4g (Saturated 1g); Cholesterol 50mg; Sodium 490mg; Carbohydrate 30g (Dietary Fiber 3g); Protein 18g • % DAILY VALUE: Vitamin A 38%; Vitamin C 22%; Calcium 4%; Iron 12% • DIET EXCHANGES: 1 Other Carbohydrate, 1/2 Fruit, 2 Vegetable, 2 Very Lean Meat, 1 Fat • CARBOHYDRATE CHOICES: 2

Chicken Fruit Salad

prep: 15 min
chill: 30 min

1/3 cup plain low-fat yogurt

2 tablespoons mayonnaise or salad dressing

I cup cubed cooked chicken

2/3 cup seedless green grapes

I large peach or nectarine, chopped (3/4 cup)

I medium stalk celery, diced (1/2 cup)

I teaspoon chopped fresh or 1/2 teaspoon dried mint leaves

1 Mix yogurt and mayonnaise in medium bowl until smooth. Stir in remaining ingredients.

2 Cover and refrigerate at least 30 minutes or until chilled.

wing it!

This fruity salad tastes best in summer when peaches or nectarines are at their peak. Serve it on lettuce leaves for salad or stuff it into a pita half for a terrific sandwich.

1 SERVING: Calories 335 (Calories from Fat 155); Fat 17g (Saturated 4g); Cholesterol 70mg; Sodium 180mg; Carbohydrate 22g (Dietary Fiber 2g); Protein 23g • % **DAILY VALUE:** Vitamin A 6%; Vitamin C 20%; Calcium 10%; Iron 6% • **DIET EXCHANGES:** I Fruit, I/2 Other Carbohydrates, 3 Medium-Fat Meat • **CARBOHYDRATE CHOICES:** I 1/2

wingit!

Keep a bag of frozen loose-pack unsweetened raspberries in your freezer so you can make this salad when fresh raspberries aren't available.

4 SERVINGS

Raspberry-Chicken Salad

Raspberry Dressing (below)

6 cups bite-size pieces mixed salad greens (such as Bibb, iceberg, romaine or spinach)

2 cups cut-up cooked chicken

I cup fresh raspberries

1/3 cup thinly sliced celery

Freshly ground pepper, if desired

1 Make Raspberry Dressing.

2 Toss salad greens, chicken, raspberries and celery. Serve with dressing and pepper.

Raspberry Dressing

I cup plain fat-free yogurt

1/2 cup fresh raspberries

I tablespoon raspberry or red wine vinegar

2 teaspoons sugar

Place all ingredients in blender. Cover and blend on high speed about 15 seconds or until smooth.

1 SERVING: Calories 195 (Calories from Fat 55); Fat 6g (Saturated 2g); Cholesterol 60mg; Sodium 135mg; Carbohydrate 15g (Dietary Fiber 5g); Protein 25g • % DAILY VALUE: Vitamin A 52%; Vitamin C 44%; Calcium 18%; Iron 12% • DIET EXCHANGES: 1/2 Fruit, I Vegetable, 2 1/2 Lean Meat • CARBOHYDRATE CHOICES: I

Raspberry-Chicken Salad

prep: 20 min

wing it!

Jicama is a large
root vegetable
with a thin brown
skin and a crisp
white flesh. This
sweet, nutty veg-
etable is delicious
raw or cooked.
Be sure to peel
the skin before
using.

4 SERVINGS

Fruited Taco Salad

Lime Cumin Vinaigrette (below)

6 cups bite-size pieces salad greens

2 cups coarsely shredded cooked chicken

1/2 cup julienne strips peeled jicama

1 medium mango, seeded and cut up

1 cup raspberries

Lime wedges, if desired

Tortilla chips, if desired

1 Make Lime Cumin Vinaigrette.

2 Toss salad greens, chicken, jicama, mango, raspberries and vinaigrette. Just before serving, lightly squeeze juice from lime wedges over salad. Serve with tortilla chips.

Lime Cumin Vinaigrette

1/4 cup olive or vegetable oil

3 tablespoons lime juice

1 tablespoon honey

1 1/2 tablespoons chopped fresh cilantro

3/4 teaspoon ground cumin

1/4 teaspoon salt

1/8 teaspoon pepper

1 to 2 cloves garlic, finely chopped

Shake all ingredients in tightly covered container.

1 SERVING: Calories 325 (Calories from Fat 170); Fat 19g (Saturated 3g); Cholesterol 60mg; Sodium 230mg; Carbohydrate 22g (Dietary Fiber 6g); Protein 22g • **% DAILY VALUE:** Vitamin A 60%; Vitamin C 70%; Calcium 6%; Iron 14% • **DIET EXCHANGES:** 1 Fruit, 1 Vegetable, 3 Medium-Fat Meat • **CARBOHYDRATE CHOICES:** 1 1/2

Fruited Taco Salad

Cantaloupe and Chicken Salad

prep: 25 min
chill: 2 hours

wing it!

Save time by purchasing cut-up cantaloupe. Honeydew or pineapple chunks can be used in place of or in addition to the cantaloupe.

1/4 cup plain yogurt

1/4 cup mayonnaise or salad dressing

1 tablespoon lemon juice

1 tablespoon chopped fresh chives

1/4 teaspoon salt

5 cups cantaloupe, cut into 1 1/2-inch pieces

2 1/2 cups cut-up cooked chicken

1 cup red or green grapes, cut in half

1 medium cucumber, cut into 1 1/4-inch strips

1 Mix yogurt and mayonnaise in large bowl. Stir in lemon juice, chives and salt.

2 Stir in remaining ingredients. Serve immediately, or refrigerate at least 2 hours until chilled but no longer than 24 hours.

1 SERVING: Calories 260 (Calories from Fat 110); Fat 12g (Saturated 2g); Cholesterol 55mg; Sodium 220mg; Carbohydrate 18g (Dietary Fiber 2g); Protein 19g • % DAILY VALUE: Vitamin A 72%; Vitamin C 100%; Calcium 4%; Iron 6% • DIET EXCHANGES: 1 Fruit, 1 Vegetable, 2 1/2 Lean Meat, 1/2 Fat • CARBOHYDRATE CHOICES: 1

Chicken Salad with Pea Pods and Almonds

1/4 cup vegetable oil

3 tablespoons sugar

2 tablespoons red wine vinegar or seasoned rice vinegar

1 tablespoon soy sauce

1/4 pound snow (Chinese) pea pods, strings removed (1 cup), cut diagonally in half

3 cups coleslaw mix

1 cup cut-up cooked chicken

1/2 cup sliced almonds, toasted

1 Mix oil, sugar, vinegar and soy sauce in large bowl.

2 Add remaining ingredients; toss. Serve immediately.

super express

prep: 15 min

wing it !

Toast nuts in an ungreased heavy skillet over medium-low heat 5 to 7 minutes, stirring frequently until browning begins, then stirring constantly until golden brown. Or bake uncovered in an ungreased shallow pan in 350° oven about 10 minutes, stirring occasionally, until golden brown.

1 **SERVING:** Calories 325 (Calories from Fat 200); Fat 22g (Saturated 3g); Cholesterol 30mg; Sodium 270mg; Carbohydrate 18g (Dietary Fiber 4g); Protein 14g • **% DAILY VALUE:** Vitamin A 2%; Vitamin C 56%; Calcium 8%; Iron 10% • **DIET EXCHANGES:** 4 Vegetable, 1 Lean Meat, 4 Fat • **CARBOHYDRATE CHOICES:** 1

Caribbean Chicken and Black Bean Salad

prep: 25 min

Spicy Lime Dressing (below)

2 cups cut-up cooked chicken

1/4 cup chopped fresh cilantro

1 large tomato, chopped (1 cup)

1 medium avocado, chopped

1 small yellow summer squash, chopped

1 can (15 ounces) black beans, rinsed and drained

Leaf lettuce

1 Make Spicy Lime Dressing.

2 Toss remaining ingredients except lettuce in large bowl. Pour dressing over salad; toss. Serve on lettuce.

Spicy Lime Dressing

1/4 cup lime juice

2 tablespoons olive or vegetable oil

1 tablespoon honey

1/2 teaspoon chili powder

1/4 teaspoon ground cumin

1/4 teaspoon salt

2 or 3 drops red pepper sauce

Shake all ingredients in tightly covered container.

wing it!

You'll get the most juice from a lime or lemon if you roll it on the counter or microwave on High 10 seconds before cutting.

1 SERVING: Calories 395 (Calories from Fat 170); Fat 19g (Saturated 4g); Cholesterol 60mg; Sodium 580mg; Carbohydrate 36g (Dietary Fiber 9g); Protein 29g • % DAILY VALUE: Vitamin A 16%; Vitamin C 32%; Calcium 8%; Iron 22% • DIET EXCHANGES: 2 Starch, 1 Vegetable, 3 Medium-Fat Meat • CARBOHYDRATE CHOICES: 2 1/2

Caribbean Chicken and Black Bean Salad

Chicken-Stuffed Tomatoes

prep: 25 min

I cup uncooked orzo or rosamarina pasta (6 ounces)

4 large tomatoes

I medium cucumber, peeled, seeded and chopped (I cup)

2 cups cut-up cooked chicken

1/2 cup ranch or creamy dill dressing

wing it!

For a nice change of pace, use 3 cups cold cooked rice instead of the pasta.

1 Cook and drain pasta as directed on package. Rinse with cold water; drain.

2 Cut stem ends from tomatoes. Remove pulp, leaving 1/2-inch wall. Chop tomato pulp; drain. Cut thin slice from bottom of each tomato to prevent tipping.

3 Mix pasta, chopped tomato and remaining ingredients. Spoon 1/2 cup pasta mixture into each tomato. Serve with remaining pasta mixture. Or cut tomato shells into halves or fourths; divide pasta mixture evenly among tomatoes.

1 SERVING: Calories 470 (Calories from Fat 180); Fat 20g (Saturated 3g); Cholesterol 70mg; Sodium 370mg; Carbohydrate 45g (Dietary Fiber 4g); Protein 28g • % DAILY VALUE: Vitamin A 28%; Vitamin C 60%; Calcium 8%; Iron 18% • DIET EXCHANGES: 2 1/2 Starch, I Vegetable, 2 Medium-Fat Meat, 2 Fat • CARBOHYDRATE CHOICES: 3

Cobb Salad

prep: 1 hr 15 min

Lemon Vinaigrette (below)

1 small head lettuce, finely shredded (6 cups)

2 cups cut-up cooked chicken

3 hard-cooked eggs, chopped

2 medium tomatoes, chopped (1 1/2 cups)

1 ripe avocado, chopped

1/4 cup crumbled blue cheese (1 ounce)

4 slices bacon, crisply cooked and crumbled

wing it!

This is a show-off salad! Instead of arranging salads on individual serving plates, arrange it on a platter or in a large, wide, shallow bowl.

1 Make Lemon Vinaigrette.

2 Divide lettuce among 4 salad plates or shallow bowls. Arrange remaining ingredients in rows on lettuce. Serve with vinaigrette.

Lemon Vinaigrette

1/2 cup vegetable oil

1/4 cup lemon juice

1 tablespoon red wine vinegar

2 teaspoons sugar

1/2 teaspoon salt

1/2 teaspoon ground mustard

1/2 teaspoon Worcestershire sauce

1/4 teaspoon pepper

1 clove garlic, finely chopped

Shake all ingredients in tightly covered container. Refrigerate at least 1 hour to blend flavors.

1 SERVING (ABOUT 3 CUPS): Calories 590 (Calories from Fat 440); Fat 49g (Saturated 10g); Cholesterol 230mg; Sodium 630mg; Carbohydrate 12g (Dietary Fiber 4g); Protein 30g • % DAILY VALUE: Vitamin A 20%; Vitamin C 36%; Calcium 10%; Iron 14% • DIET EXCHANGES: 4 High-Fat Meat, 2 Vegetable, 3 Fat • CARBOHYDRATE CHOICES: 1

wing it!

**Hail Caesar!
Make this classic
in a snap and use
a couple of bags
of romaine or a
romaine lettuce
blend.**

6 SERVINGS

Quick Chicken Caesar Salad

3 cups cut-up cooked chicken

1 large or 2 small bunches romaine, torn into bite-size pieces (10 cups)

1 1/2 cups Caesar or garlic-flavored croutons

1/3 cup freshly grated Parmesan cheese

Freshly ground pepper

2/3 cup Caesar dressing

1 Place chicken, romaine, croutons, cheese and pepper in large bowl.

2 Toss with dressing until coated.

1 SERVING: Calories 305 (Calories from Fat 160); Fat 18g (Saturated 5g); Cholesterol 75mg; Sodium 540mg; Carbohydrate 10g (Dietary Fiber 2g); Protein 24g • **% DAILY VALUE:** Vitamin A 40%; Vitamin C 36%; Calcium 14%; Iron 12% • **DIET EXCHANGES:** 2 Vegetable, 3 Medium-Fat Meat, 1/2 Fat • **CARBOHYDRATE CHOICES:** 1/2

Quick Chicken Caesar Salad

prep: 20 min

wing it!

Sausalito is a quaint town across the bay from San Francisco that's known for its outdoor cafes and wonderful seafood. This salad will transport you there!

4 SERVINGS

Sausalito Chicken and Seafood Salad

6 cups bite-size pieces assorted salad greens

1 cup diced cooked chicken

1 large avocado, sliced

1 package (8 ounces) refrigerated imitation crabmeat chunks

1 can (4 1/2 ounces) whole green chiles, drained and sliced lengthwise

1 container (6 ounces) frozen guacamole, thawed

1/2 cup sour cream

1 large tomato, chopped (1 cup)

Lime or lemon wedges

1 Divide salad greens among 4 individual plates. Top with chicken, avocado, crabmeat and chiles.

2 Mix guacamole and sour cream; spoon over salad. Top with tomato. Garnish with lime wedges.

1 SERVING: Calories 305 (Calories from Fat 170); Fat 19g (Saturated 6g); Cholesterol 65mg; Sodium 700mg; Carbohydrate 16g (Dietary Fiber 6g); Protein 23g • **% DAILY VALUE:** Vitamin A 66%; Vitamin C 74%; Calcium 8%; Iron 14% • **DIET EXCHANGES:** 3 Vegetable, 2 1/2 Lean Meat, 1 Fat • **CARBOHYDRATE CHOICES:** 1

Tossed Chef's Salad

prep: **30 min**

1/2 cup julienne strips cooked meat (beef, pork or smoked ham)

1/2 cup julienne strips cooked chicken

1/2 cup julienne strips Swiss cheese

8 medium green onions, chopped (1/2 cup)

1 medium head lettuce, torn into bite-size pieces (10 cups)

1 small bunch romaine, torn into bite-size pieces (6 cups)

1 medium stalk celery, sliced (1/2 cup)

1/2 cup mayonnaise or salad dressing

1/4 cup French dressing

2 hard-cooked eggs, sliced

2 medium tomatoes, cut into wedges

1 Reserve a few strips of meat, chicken and cheese for topping salad. Mix remaining meat, chicken and cheese, the onions, lettuce, romaine and celery in large bowl.

2 Mix mayonnaise and French dressing. Pour over lettuce mixture; toss. Top with reserved meat, chicken and cheese strips, the eggs and tomatoes. Store remaining salad covered in refrigerator.

wingit!

There's plenty of room for inspiration. Use any cheese in place of the Swiss. Or try leeks instead of the green onions.

1 SERVING: Calories 385 (Calories from Fat 270); Fat 30g (Saturated 7g); Cholesterol 130mg; Sodium 540mg; Carbohydrate 12g (Dietary Fiber 4g); Protein 16g • % DAILY VALUE: Vitamin A 52%; Vitamin C 60%; Calcium 20%; Iron 14% • DIET EXCHANGES: 2 Vegetable, 1 1/2 High-Fat Meat, 4 Fat • CARBOHYDRATE CHOICES: 1

Garden Vegetables, Chicken and Pasta Salad

prep: 15 min
chill: 10 min

wing it !

Want a twist on this main dish? Try using frozen creamy Cheddar vegetables with pasta or garlic-seasoned vegetables with pasta.

I bag (16 ounces) frozen garden herb vegetables with pasta

I cup shredded cooked chicken

2 medium stalks celery, sliced (1 cup)

1/4 cup ranch dressing

Freshly ground pepper, if desired

1 Cook vegetables as directed on package.

2 Stir in chicken, celery and dressing. Cover and refrigerate 10 minutes to cool. Sprinkle with pepper.

1 SERVING: Calories 265 (Calories from Fat 90); Fat 10g (Saturated 1g); Cholesterol 35mg; Sodium 650mg; Carbohydrate 28g (Dietary Fiber 4g); Protein 16g • % DAILY VALUE: Vitamin A 48%; Vitamin C 48%; Calcium 6%; Iron 10% • DIET EXCHANGES: I Starch, 2 Vegetable, I 1/2 Medium-Fat Meat, 1/2 Fat • CARBOHYDRATE CHOICES: 2

Garden Vegetables, Chicken and Pasta Salad

super express

wing it!

This is the perfect salad to toss together when you invite last-minute guests over—it's fast, but special. A quick stop at the store for tortellini, salad greens and a rotisserie chicken and you're ready to cook.

6 SERVINGS

Chicken and Tortellini Salad

1 package (9 ounces) refrigerated cheese-filled tortellini

6 cups bite-size pieces assorted salad greens

3 cups chopped cooked chicken

1/2 cup Italian dressing

1/3 cup shredded Parmesan cheese

1 Cook and drain tortellini as directed on package.

2 Mix tortellini and remaining ingredients except cheese. Sprinkle with cheese.

1 SERVING: Calories 310 (Calories from Fat 160); Fat 18g (Saturated 4g); Cholesterol 105mg; Sodium 380mg; Carbohydrate 11g (Dietary Fiber 1g); Protein 26g • **% DAILY VALUE:** Vitamin A 38%; Vitamin C 16%; Calcium 16%; Iron 12% • **DIET EXCHANGES:** 1/2 Starch, 1 Vegetable, 3 Lean Meat, 2 Fat • **CARBOHYDRATE CHOICES:** 1

4 SERVINGS

Chicken-Pasta Salad with Pesto

prep: 20 min

2 1/4 cups uncooked multicolored farfalle (bow-tie) pasta (6 ounces)

1 1/2 cups cut-up cooked chicken

1/4 cup oil-packed sun-dried tomatoes, drained and chopped

1 medium bell pepper, cut into 1/4-inch strips

1 small zucchini, thinly sliced

1/2 small red onion, sliced

1/3 cup prepared pesto

1 Cook pasta as directed on package; drain. Rinse with cold water; drain.

2 Mix pasta, chicken, tomatoes, bell pepper, zucchini and onion in large bowl. Stir in pesto.

wing it!

Presto pesto—buy it already made. You'll have leftover pesto, so store it in the fridge and toss it with hot cooked pasta for another easy meal.

1 SERVING: Calories 400 (Calories from Fat 155); Fat 17g (Saturated 3g); Cholesterol 50mg; Sodium 250mg; Carbohydrate 39g (Dietary Fiber 3g); Protein 23g • % **DAILY VALUE:** Vitamin A 12%; Vitamin C 62%; Calcium 10%; Iron 18% • **DIET EXCHANGES:** 2 Starch, 2 Vegetable, 1 1/2 Medium-Fat Meat, 2 Fat • **CARBOHYDRATE CHOICES:** 2 1/2

Chicken-Curry-Couscous Salad

prep: **25 min**
chill: **1 hr**

wing it!

Create a Middle Eastern luncheon by serving this salad with flatbread or pita breads.

Curry Dressing (below)

2 cups cooked couscous

1 cup diced cooked chicken

1 cup raisins

1 medium red or yellow bell pepper, cut into thin strips

6 medium green onions, chopped (6 tablespoons)

1 can (15 to 16 ounces) garbanzo beans, rinsed and drained

1/2 cup chopped roasted almonds

1 Make Curry Dressing.

2 Place remaining ingredients except almonds in large bowl. Pour dressing over salad; toss until coated. Cover and refrigerate about 1 hour or until chilled. Top with almonds.

Curry Dressing

1/3 cup light olive or vegetable oil

1 tablespoon lemon juice

1 teaspoon sugar

1/2 teaspoon curry powder

1/4 teaspoon salt

1/8 teaspoon ground allspice

Shake all ingredients in tightly covered container.

1 SERVING: Calories 740 (Calories from Fat 295); Fat 33g (Saturated 4g); Cholesterol 30mg; Sodium 380mg; Carbohydrate 88g (Dietary Fiber 13g); Protein 36g • % DAILY VALUE: Vitamin A 38%; Vitamin C 100%; Calcium 16%; Iron 34% • DIET EXCHANGES: 5 Starch, 2 Vegetable, 2 1/2 Medium-Fat Meat, 2 Fat • CARBOHYDRATE CHOICES: 6

Chicken-Curry-Couscous Salad

wing it!

This salad is as simple as heating chicken broth. All you have to do is heat the broth to boiling, then stir in the couscous, and toss it with the other ingredients.

6 SERVINGS

Italian Chicken-Couscous Salad

2 cups ready-to-serve chicken broth

1 1/3 cups uncooked couscous

1 bag (16 ounces) frozen broccoli, red pepper, onions and mushrooms, thawed

3 cups cubed cooked chicken

1 bottle (8 ounces) fat-free creamy Italian dressing (3/4 cup)

Lettuce leaves, if desired

1 Heat broth to boiling in 1 1/2-quart saucepan; reduce heat. Stir in couscous; remove from heat. Cover and let stand 5 minutes.

2 Mix couscous, vegetables and chicken in large bowl. Pour dressing over mixture; toss lightly to coat. Line 6 salad plates with lettuce. Spoon salad onto lettuce.

1 SERVING: Calories 350 (Calories from Fat 55); Fat 6g (Saturated 2g); Cholesterol 60mg; Sodium 1120mg; Carbohydrate 45g (Dietary Fiber 4g); Protein 29g • **% DAILY VALUE:** Vitamin A 16%; Vitamin C 46%; Calcium 4%; Iron 12% • **DIET EXCHANGES:** 2 Starch, 3 Vegetable, 2 Lean Meat • **CARBOHYDRATE CHOICES:** 3

Italian Chopped Salad

prep: 30 min

Basil Vinaigrette (below)

6 cups chopped romaine

1 cup fresh basil leaves

1 cup cut-up cooked chicken

2 large tomatoes, chopped (2 cups)

2 medium cucumbers, chopped (1 1/2 cups)

1 package (3 ounces) Italian salami, chopped

1 can (15 to 16 ounces) cannellini beans, rinsed and drained

1 Make Basil Vinaigrette.

2 Place remaining ingredients in large bowl. Pour vinaigrette over salad; toss until coated.

Basil Vinaigrette

1/3 cup vegetable oil

1/4 cup red wine vinegar

2 tablespoons chopped fresh or 2 teaspoons dried basil leaves

1 teaspoon sugar

1/4 teaspoon salt

Shake all ingredients in tightly covered container.

wing it!

You can find many versions of chopped salads in restaurants today that can be eaten as salad, vegetable and salsa all at once. This is a main-dish version you'll love. Sprinkle salad with shredded Romano or Parmesan cheese too.

1 SERVING: Calories 380 (Calories from Fat 260); Fat 29g (Saturated 6g); Cholesterol 45mg; Sodium 830mg; Carbohydrate 16g (Dietary Fiber 5g); Protein 19g • % DAILY VALUE: Vitamin A 82%; Vitamin C 78%; Calcium 10%; Iron 20% • DIET EXCHANGES: 1/2 Starch, 2 Vegetable, 2 Medium-Fat Meat, 3 Fat • CARBOHYDRATE CHOICES: 1

super express

wing it!

The choices for salad dressings are endless. Try zesty Italian, Parmesan ranch, red wine vinaigrette or garlic ranch.

6 SERVINGS

Mediterranean Chicken Salad

2 cups diced cooked chicken

1 bag (10 ounces) ready-to-eat Italian-blend salad greens

1 can (14 ounces) artichoke hearts, drained and chopped

1 can (4 1/4 ounces) chopped ripe olives, drained

1/4 cup tomato-and-herb Italian dressing

1 Mix all ingredients except dressing in large bowl.

2 Add dressing; toss until coated.

1 SERVING: Calories 185 (Calories from Fat 80); Fat 9g (Saturated 2g); Cholesterol 40mg; Sodium 450mg; Carbohydrate 10g (Dietary Fiber 5g); Protein 16g • % DAILY VALUE: Vitamin A 32%; Vitamin C 22%; Calcium 8%; Iron 12% • DIET EXCHANGES: 2 Vegetable, 2 Medium-Fat Meat • CARBOHYDRATE CHOICES: 1/2

Mediterranean Chicken Salad

wing it!

If you can't find the Oriental-flavored ramen noodle soup mix, go ahead and use any ramen noodle soup mix such as teriyaki chicken— or for a little more flavor— Cajun chicken or spicy chili chicken.

6 SERVINGS

Crunchy Oriental Chicken Salad

2 tablespoons butter or margarine

1 package (3 ounces) Oriental-flavor ramen noodle soup mix

2 tablespoons sesame seed

1/4 cup sugar

1/4 cup white vinegar

1 tablespoon sesame or vegetable oil

1/2 teaspoon pepper

2 cups cut-up cooked chicken

1/4 cup dry-roasted peanuts, if desired

4 medium green onions, sliced (1/4 cup)

1 bag (16 ounces) coleslaw mix

1 can (11 ounces) mandarin orange segments, drained

1 Melt butter in 10-inch skillet over medium heat. Stir in seasoning packet from soup mix. Break block of noodles into bite-size pieces over skillet; stir into butter mixture.

2 Cook 2 minutes, stirring occasionally. Stir in sesame seed. Cook about 2 minutes longer, stirring occasionally, until noodles are golden brown; remove from heat.

3 Mix sugar, vinegar, oil and pepper in large bowl. Add noodle mixture and remaining ingredients; toss.

1 SERVING: Calories 300 (Calories from Fat 125); Fat 14g (Saturated 5g); Cholesterol 50mg; Sodium 320mg; Carbohydrate 26g (Dietary Fiber 3g); Protein 17g • % DAILY VALUE: Vitamin A 10%; Vitamin C 62%; Calcium 6%; Iron 10% • DIET EXCHANGES: 1 Starch, 2 Vegetable, 1 1/2 Medium-Fat Meat, 1 1/2 Fat • CARBOHYDRATE CHOICES: 2

6 SERVINGS

Asian Chicken Salad with Peanut-Soy Dressing

prep: **20 min**

Peanut-Soy Dressing (below)

6 cups coleslaw mix

3 cups washed fresh spinach leaves (from 10-ounce bag)

3 cups chopped cooked chicken

1 medium bell pepper, thinly sliced

1 can (8 ounces) bamboo shoots, rinsed and drained

1 Make Peanut-Soy Dressing.

2 Toss remaining ingredients in large bowl. Drizzle with dressing. Serve immediately.

Peanut-Soy Dressing

3 tablespoons reduced-sodium soy sauce

3 tablespoons cider vinegar

2 tablespoons honey

1 tablespoon creamy peanut butter

1/2 teaspoon crushed red pepper

1/2 teaspoon grated gingerroot

Beat all ingredients with wire whisk until blended.

wing it!

Soy sauces can vary greatly in color from light to dark and texture from thin to thick, so pick your favorite. Explore an Asian market, and experiment with different varieties.

1 SERVING: Calories 215 (Calories from Fat 65); Fat 7g (Saturated 2g); Cholesterol 60mg; Sodium 370mg; Carbohydrate 15g (Dietary Fiber 4g); Protein 23g • % DAILY VALUE: Vitamin A 34%; Vitamin C 84%; Calcium 6%; Iron 12% • DIET EXCHANGES: 3 Vegetable, 2 Lean Meat, 1/2 Fat • CARBOHYDRATE CHOICES: 1

Chopped Chicken Asian Salad

prep: 30 min

wingit!

Escarole is one of three main varieties of endive. It has broad, slightly curved, pale green leaves and is the mildest of the endive family. If you prefer, for an even milder flavor, you can use romaine in place of the escarole.

Lime Dressing (below)

2 cups chopped escarole

1 cup chopped cooked chicken

1 small jicama, peeled and chopped (1 cup)

1 large papaya, peeled and chopped (1 cup)

1 medium yellow or red bell pepper, chopped (1 cup)

1/2 cup dry-roasted peanuts

1/4 cup chopped cilantro

1 Make Lime Dressing.

2 Place remaining ingredients except peanuts and cilantro in large bowl. Pour dressing over salad; toss until coated. Top with peanuts and cilantro.

Lime Dressing

1/3 cup frozen (thawed) limeade

1/4 cup vegetable oil

1 tablespoon rice or white vinegar

1 teaspoon grated gingerroot

1/4 teaspoon salt

Shake all ingredients in tightly covered container.

1 SERVING: Calories 410 (Calories from Fat 235); Fat 26g (Saturated 4g); Cholesterol 30mg; Sodium 340mg; Carbohydrate 36g (Dietary Fiber 9g); Protein 17g • % DAILY VALUE: Vitamin A 30%; Vitamin C 100%; Calcium 6%; Iron 10% • DIET EXCHANGES: 1 Fruit, 1/2 Other Carbohydrate, 2 Vegetable, 2 Medium-Fat Meat, 2 1/2 Fat • CARBOHYDRATE CHOICES: 2 1/2

Chopped Chicken Asian Salad

Asian Chicken-Manicotti Salad

prep: 25 min

wing it!

Bottled peanut sauce is readily available in most supermarkets. If you're in a hurry, instead of making the dressing, you can use peanut sauce and thin it with a little vinegar and oil.

Tangy Peanut Dressing (below)

8 uncooked manicotti shells

5 cups coleslaw mix

1 1/2 cups finely chopped cooked chicken

1 cup bean sprouts, finely chopped

1/2 cup peanuts, chopped

1/4 cup canned water chestnuts, chopped

1 Make Tangy Peanut Dressing. Cook and drain manicotti shells as directed on package. Rinse with cold water; drain.

2 Finely chop 1 cup of the coleslaw mix. Mix finely chopped coleslaw, the chicken, bean sprouts, peanuts and water chestnuts.

3 Fill each cooked shell with chicken mixture. Divide remaining coleslaw mix among 4 individual plates. Top each with manicotti. Drizzle with dressing.

Tangy Peanut Dressing

1/3 cup vegetable oil

2 tablespoons rice or white vinegar

2 tablespoons creamy peanut butter

1 tablespoon soy sauce

1/8 teaspoon ground red pepper (cayenne)

1 clove garlic, finely chopped

Mix all ingredients with wire whisk.

1 SERVING: Calories 590 (Calories from Fat 335); Fat 37g (Saturated 6g); Cholesterol 45mg; Sodium 540mg; Carbohydrate 40g (Dietary Fiber 6g); Protein 30g • **% DAILY VALUE:** Vitamin A 4%; Vitamin C 66%; Calcium 10%; Iron 20% • **DIET EXCHANGES:** 2 Starch, 2 Vegetable, 3 Medium-Fat Meat, 3 1/2 Fat • **CARBOHYDRATE CHOICES:** 2 1/2

Asian Chicken-Manicotti Salad

prep: **20 min**

wing it!

Go ahead and use packaged, assorted pre-washed salad greens for this recipe to save time.

4 SERVINGS

Thai Chicken Salad

Honey-Ginger Dressing (below)

6 cups bite-size pieces assorted salad greens

1 1/2 cups shredded cooked chicken

1 medium carrot, shredded (3/4 cup)

1 can (14 to 15 ounces) baby corn nuggets, drained

1/3 cup flaked coconut, toasted

1 Make Honey-Ginger Dressing.

2 Place salad greens, chicken, carrot and corn in large bowl. Pour dressing over salad; toss until coated. Sprinkle with coconut.

Honey-Ginger Dressing

1/4 cup vegetable oil

2 tablespoons balsamic or cider vinegar

2 tablespoons soy sauce

1 tablespoon honey

1 teaspoon grated gingerroot

Shake all ingredients in tightly covered container.

1 **SERVING:** Calories 375 (Calories from Fat 190); Fat 21g (Saturated 5g); Cholesterol 45mg; Sodium 750mg; Carbohydrate 32g (Dietary Fiber 4g); Protein 19g • % **DAILY VALUE:** Vitamin A 32%; Vitamin C 26%; Calcium 4%; Iron 14% • **DIET EXCHANGES:** 1 Starch, 1 1/2 Lean Meat, 3 Vegetable, 3 Fat • **CARBOHYDRATE CHOICES:** 2

Thai Chicken Salad

Chicken and Wild Rice Salad with Dried Cherries

prep: 25 min

wing it!

Transform this salad into a masterpiece. Add 1/2 cup chopped dried apricots. Turn up the heat by sprinkling in 1/4 teaspoon crushed red pepper.

1 package (6.2 ounces) fast-cooking long-grain and wild rice mix

1 cup diced cooked chicken

1 medium unpeeled eating apple, chopped (1 cup)

1 medium green bell pepper, chopped (1 cup)

1 medium stalk celery, chopped (1/2 cup)

1/3 cup dried cherries, chopped

2 tablespoons reduced-sodium soy sauce

2 tablespoons water

2 teaspoons sugar

2 teaspoons cider vinegar

1/3 cup dry-roasted peanuts

1 Cook rice mix as directed on package, except omit butter. Spread rice evenly in thin layer on large cookie sheet. Let stand 10 minutes, stirring occasionally, until cool.

2 Mix chicken, apple, bell pepper, celery and cherries in large bowl.

3 Mix soy sauce, water, sugar and vinegar in small bowl until sugar is dissolved. Add rice and soy sauce mixture to apple mixture. Gently toss until coated. Add peanuts; gently toss.

1 SERVING: Calories 180 (Calories from Fat 55); Fat 6g (Saturated 1g); Cholesterol 20mg; Sodium 380mg; Carbohydrate 22g (Dietary Fiber 2g); Protein 10g • % DAILY VALUE: Vitamin A 2%; Vitamin C 34%; Calcium 2%; Iron 6% • DIET EXCHANGES: 1 Starch, 1 Vegetable, 1/2 Lean Meat, 1 Fat • CARBOHYDRATE CHOICES: 1 1/2

Chicken and Wild Rice Salad with Dried Cherries

Wild Rice–Chicken Salad with Raspberry Vinaigrette

prep: 15 min
chill: 1 hr

wing it!

Jazz it up! For a nutty flavor, toss chopped walnuts or pecans into this salad. For extra color add dried cherries or cranberries.

3 cups cold cooked wild rice

1 1/2 cups cubed cooked chicken

4 medium green onions, chopped (4 tablespoons)

1 medium green bell pepper, chopped (1 cup)

1 can (8 ounces) sliced water chestnuts, drained

1 package (6 ounces) diced dried fruits and raisins

1/3 cup raspberry vinegar

1/4 cup honey

2 tablespoons vegetable oil

1 Mix all ingredients except vinegar, honey and oil in large bowl.

2 Shake vinegar, honey and oil in tightly covered container. Pour over wild rice mixture; toss.

3 Cover and refrigerate 1 to 2 hours to blend flavors.

1 SERVING: Calories 345 (Calories from Fat 70); Fat 8g (Saturated 1g); Cholesterol 30mg; Sodium 320mg; Carbohydrate 54g (Dietary Fiber 4g); Protein 14g • % DAILY VALUE: Vitamin A 8%; Vitamin C 36%; Calcium 4%; Iron 12% • DIET EXCHANGES: 2 Starch, 1 Fruit, 2 Vegetable, 1 Lean Meat • CARBOHYDRATE CHOICES: 3 1/2

4 Suddenly Sandwiches and Pizzas

◐ = **super express** ready in 20 minutes or less

prep: 15 min

wing it!

Zest it up! Toss sprigs of fresh cilantro on top of the filling, then roll 'em up.

6 SANDWICHES

Adobe Chicken Wrap

1 1/2 cups chopped cooked chicken

1/2 cup salsa

1 can (15 to 16 ounces) black beans, rinsed and drained

1 can (8 3/4 ounces) whole kernel corn, drained

6 spinach or regular flour tortillas (8 to 10 inches in diameter)

1/3 cup sour cream

Salsa, if desired

1 Mix chicken, 1/2 cup salsa, the beans and corn. Divide chicken mixture among tortillas, spreading to within 2 inches of bottom of each tortilla. Top each with sour cream.

2 Fold one end of the tortilla up about 1 inch over filling; fold right and left sides over folded end, overlapping. Fold remaining end down. Serve with salsa.

1 SERVING: Calories 325 (Calories from Fat 80); Fat 9g (Saturated 3g); Cholesterol 40mg; Sodium 625mg; Carbohydrate 47g (Dietary Fiber 7g); Protein 20g • % DAILY VALUE: Vitamin A 4%; Vitamin C 10%; Calcium 12%; Iron 20% • DIET EXCHANGES: 3 Starch, 1 Medium-Fat Meat, 1 Fat • CARBOHYDRATE CHOICES: 3

Chicken Gyro Wrap

 super *express*

prep: **10 min**

1 1/2 cups chopped cooked chicken

1/2 cup chopped lettuce

1/4 cup diced red onion

1 medium cucumber, finely chopped (1 cup)

4 flour tortillas (8 to 10 inches in diameter)

8 tablespoons cucumber ranch dressing

1 Mix chicken, lettuce, onion and cucumber. Divide chicken mixture among tortillas, spreading to within 2 inches of bottom of each tortilla. Top each with 2 tablespoons dressing.

2 Fold one end of tortilla up about 1 inch over filling; fold right and left sides over folded end, overlapping. Fold remaining end down. Cut in half to serve.

wing it!

Increase the fun by trying other flavors of tortillas, such as red pepper, herb or tomato.

1 **SERVING:** Calories 405 (Calories from Fat 205); Fat 23g (Saturated 4g); Cholesterol 45mg; Sodium 455mg; Carbohydrate 30g (Dietary Fiber 2g); Protein 20g • % **DAILY VALUE:** Vitamin A 4%; Vitamin C 4%; Calcium 8%; Iron 12% • **DIET EXCHANGES:** 2 Starch, 2 Lean Meat, 3 Fat • **CARBOHYDRATE CHOICES:** 2

wing it!

For a fresh summer sandwich bursting with flavor, top each tortilla with 2 tablespoons of sliced strawberries before rolling up into a wrap.

4 SERVINGS

Cranberry-Chicken Wrap

4 fat-free flour tortillas (6 to 8 inches in diameter)

1/2 tub (8-ounce size) reduced-fat cream cheese (Neufchâtel) (1/2 cup)

1/4 cup jellied cranberry sauce or strawberry spreadable fruit

2 teaspoons mustard

1 1/2 cups chopped cooked chicken

1/2 cup shredded reduced-fat mozzarella cheese (2 ounces)

1/2 cup alfalfa sprouts, if desired

1 Spread each tortilla with 2 tablespoons cream cheese, 1 tablespoon cranberry sauce and 1/2 teaspoon mustard. Sprinkle with chicken, mozzarella cheese and sprouts.

2 Fold one end of each tortilla up about 1 inch over filling; fold right and left sides over folded end, overlapping. Fold remaining end down.

1 SANDWICH: Calories 355 (Calories from Fat 125); Fat 13g (Saturated 7g); Cholesterol 75mg; Sodium 380mg; Carbohydrate 22g (Dietary Fiber 1g); Protein 24g • % DAILY VALUE: Vitamin A 8%; Vitamin C 0%; Calcium 16%; Iron 8% • DIET EXCHANGES: 1 1/2 Starch, 3 Medium-Fat Meat • CARBOHYDRATE CHOICES: 1 1/2

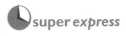

6 SERVINGS

Dressy French Chicken Sandwiches

prep: 15 min
cook: 5 min

2 cups cubed cooked chicken

1/2 cup chopped red bell pepper (about 1 small)

1/2 cup chopped cucumber

1/2 cup shredded mozzarella cheese (2 ounces)

1/2 cup mayonnaise or salad dressing

2 teaspoons chopped fresh or 1/2 teaspoon dried oregano leaves

1 can (4 1/4 ounces) chopped ripe olives, drained

1 baguette (14 to 16 inches), cut horizontally in half

wing it!

The good news—many supermarket bakeries carry excellent baguettes. However, if you can't find them, just use regular French bread.

1 Set oven control to broil.

2 Mix all ingredients except baguette. Spoon about 1 1/2 cups chicken mixture onto each bread half.

3 Place on ungreased cookie sheet. Broil with tops 4 to 6 inches from heat about 5 minutes or until hot. Cut each into 3 slices.

1 SERVING: Calories 435 (Calories from Fat 205); Fat 23g (Saturated 5g); Cholesterol 55mg; Sodium 690mg; Carbohydrate 35g (Dietary Fiber 3g); Protein 22g • **% DAILY VALUE:** Vitamin A 18%; Vitamin C 20%; Calcium 14%; Iron 16% • **DIET EXCHANGES:** 2 Starch, 1 Vegetable, 2 Medium-Fat Meat, 2 Fat • **CARBOHYDRATE CHOICES:** 2

Baked Chicken, Cheddar and Bacon Sandwich

prep: **15 min**
bake: **32 min**
stand: **5 min**

wingit!

This hot sandwich has all the delicious flavors of a club sandwich. Invite your family to "join the club" around the table!

2 cups Original Bisquick mix

1 cup milk

1 egg

6 slices chicken breast

1 1/2 cups shredded Cheddar cheese (6 ounces)

5 slices cooked bacon

1 Heat oven to 400°. Spray square baking dish, 8 × 8 × 2 inches, with cooking spray.

2 Stir Bisquick mix, milk and egg until blended. Spread half of the batter in baking dish. Top with chicken, 1 cup of the cheese and the bacon. Spread remaining batter over bacon.

3 Bake uncovered about 29 minutes or until golden brown and center is set. Sprinkle with remaining 1/2 cup cheese. Bake about 3 minutes or until cheese is melted. Let stand 5 minutes before cutting.

1 SERVING: Calories 380 (Calories from Fat 180); Fat 20g (Saturated 9g); Cholesterol 90mg; Sodium 875mg; Carbohydrate 27g (Dietary Fiber 0g); Protein 19g • **% DAILY VALUE:** Vitamin A 8%; Vitamin C 0%; Calcium 26%; Iron 10% • **DIET EXCHANGES:** 2 Starch, 1/2 Medium-Fat Meat, 2 Fat • **CARBOHYDRATE CHOICES:** 2

Baked Chicken, Cheddar and Bacon Sandwich

Chicken Mini-Sandwiches

prep: 15 min
bake: 50 min
stand: 5 min

wing it !

Make it easier on yourself! Bake these sandwiches the day before and cut into serving pieces. Store covered in the refrigerator, and serve cold the next day. Or to serve warm, place serving pieces on a cookie sheet, cover loosely with aluminum foil and reheat in 350° oven about 10 minutes or until warm.

2 cups **Original Bisquick mix**
1/2 cup **dried cranberries**
1 cup **milk**
2 tablespoons **yellow mustard**

1 **egg**
1 cup **chopped cooked chicken**
1 cup **shredded Swiss cheese (4 ounces)**

1 Heat oven to 350°. Spray bottom and sides of square baking dish, 8 × 8 × 2 inches, with cooking spray.

2 Stir Bisquick mix, cranberries, milk, mustard and egg until blended. Pour half of the batter into baking dish. Top with half of the chicken; sprinkle with 1/2 cup of the cheese to within 1/4 inch of edges of baking dish. Top with remaining chicken. Pour remaining batter over chicken.

3 Bake uncovered 45 to 50 minutes or until golden brown and set. Sprinkle with remaining 1/2 cup cheese. Let stand 5 minutes before cutting. Cut into 9 squares; cut each square diagonally in half.

1 MINI-SANDWICH: Calories 115 (Calories from Fat 45); Fat 5g (Saturated 2g); Cholesterol 25mg; Sodium 240mg; Carbohydrate 12g (Dietary Fiber 0g); Protein 5g • % DAILY VALUE: Vitamin A 2%; Vitamin C 0%; Calcium 10%; Iron 2% • DIET EXCHANGES: 1 Starch, 1 Fat • CARBOHYDRATE CHOICES: 1

Chicken Mini-Sandwiches

Chicken Quesadilla Sandwiches

prep: 30 min
cook: 24 min

wing it!

For a super-quick rice dish to serve with the quesadillas, combine hot cooked rice with salsa or with melted process cheese spread. Top with sliced ripe olives and chopped green onions for a festive look.

1 1/2 cups shredded cooked chicken

1/4 cup chopped fresh cilantro

1/4 teaspoon ground cumin

8 flour tortillas (8 to 10 inches in diameter)

Cooking spray

1 cup shredded Monterey Jack cheese (4 ounces)

1 can (4 1/2 ounces) chopped green chiles, drained

Salsa, if desired

1 Mix together chicken with cilantro and cumin

2 Spray 1 side of 1 tortilla with cooking spray; place sprayed side down in skillet. Layer with one-fourth of the chicken mixture, 1/4 cup of the cheese and one-fourth of the chiles to within 1/2 inch of edge of tortilla. Top with another tortilla; spray top of tortilla with cooking spray.

3 Cook over medium-high heat 4 to 6 minutes, turning after 2 minutes, until light golden brown. Repeat with remaining tortillas, chicken mixture, cheese and chiles. Cut quesadillas into wedges. Serve with salsa.

1 **SERVING:** Calories 470 (Calories from Fat 160); Fat 18g (Saturated 8g); Cholesterol 70mg; Sodium 680mg; Carbohydrate 49g (Dietary Fiber 3g); Protein 29g • % **DAILY VALUE:** Vitamin A 8%; Vitamin C 46%; Calcium 32%; Iron 22% • **DIET EXCHANGES:** 3 Starch, 3 Medium-Fat Meat • **CARBOHYDRATE CHOICES:** 3

Chicken Quesadilla Sandwiches

prep: **20 min**
cook: **5 min**

Easy Chicken Fajitas

wing**it!**

Make an everyday meal extraordinary with a build-your-own-fajita buffet. Set out colorful bowls filled with the tomato, cheese, lettuce, sour cream and salsa. Add guacamole, sliced ripe olives and chopped fresh cilantro as well.

1 medium onion, sliced

2 tablespoons Mexican seasoning

2 tablespoons vegetable oil

2 cups chopped cooked chicken

8 flour tortillas (6 inches in diameter)

1 medium tomato, chopped (3/4 cup)

1 cup shredded Cheddar cheese (4 ounces)

1 cup shredded lettuce

1/2 cup sour cream

1/2 cup salsa

1 Place onion, Mexican seasoning and oil in large bowl; toss.

2 Heat 12-inch skillet over medium-high heat; add onion mixture. Cook about 4 minutes, stirring frequently, until onion is crisp-tender. Stir in chicken. Cook about 1 minute or until heated through.

3 Divide chicken mixture among tortillas. Sprinkle with tomato and cheese. Add lettuce, sour cream and salsa. Roll up tortillas.

1 SERVING: Calories 500 (Calories from Fat 215); Fat 24g (Saturated 12g); Cholesterol 110mg; Sodium 850mg; Carbohydrate 38g (Dietary Fiber 4g); Protein 33g • **% DAILY VALUE:** Vitamin A 30%; Vitamin C 12%; Calcium 28%; Iron 20% • **DIET EXCHANGES:** 2 Starch, 2 Vegetable, 3 Medium-Fat Meat, 1 1/2 Fat • **CARBOHYDRATE CHOICES:** 2 1/2

Easy Chicken Fajitas

Chicken Tacos

prep: 25 min

wing it!

Perfectly ripe avocados are silky smooth and have the best flavor. Avocados are ripe and ready to use when they yield to gentle pressure but still feel slightly firm.

1 small avocado	10 taco shells
Lemon juice	2 cups shredded Monterey Jack cheese (8 ounces)
2 tablespoons vegetable oil	1/3 cup sliced pimiento-stuffed olives
2 cups chopped cooked chicken	1 cup shredded lettuce
1 can (4 1/2 ounces) chopped green chiles, drained	Taco sauce, if desired
1 small onion, sliced	Sour cream, if desired

1 Cut avocado in half; remove pit and avocado peel. Cut halves into slices. Sprinkle with lemon juice to keep avocado from turning brown.

2 Heat oil in 10-inch skillet over medium heat. Cook chicken, chiles and onion in oil, stirring occasionally, until chicken is hot. Heat taco shells as directed on package.

3 Spoon about 1/4 cup chicken mixture into each shell. Top with cheese, olives, lettuce and avocado. Serve with taco sauce and sour cream.

1 SERVING: Calories 530 (Calories from Fat 325); Fat 36g (Saturated 12g); Cholesterol 90mg; Sodium 680mg; Carbohydrate 22g (Dietary Fiber 4g); Protein 30g • % DAILY VALUE: Vitamin A 14%; Vitamin C 14%; Calcium 40%; Iron 14% • DIET EXCHANGES: 1 1/2 Starch, 3 1/2 Medium-Fat Meat, 3 1/2 Fat • CARBOHYDRATE CHOICES: 1 1/2

Corn Bread Chili Stacks

prep: **15 min**
bake: **20 min**

3/4 cup yellow cornmeal

2/3 cup **Original Bisquick mix**

3/4 cup buttermilk

2 tablespoons butter or margarine, melted

1 egg

1 can (15 ounces) spicy chili

1 can (10 ounces) diced tomatoes with mild green chiles, undrained

1 cup cut-up cooked chicken

4 slices American cheese, cut diagonally in half, if desired

1 Heat oven to 450°. Spray bottom and sides of square pan, 8 × 8 × 2 inches, with cooking spray. Stir cornmeal, Bisquick mix, buttermilk, butter and egg in medium bowl until blended. Pour into pan.

2 Bake uncovered 18 to 20 minutes or until toothpick inserted in center comes out clean. Meanwhile, heat chili, tomatoes and chicken in 2-quart saucepan over medium heat, stirring occasionally, until bubbly.

3 Cut corn bread into 4 squares; split each square horizontally. Fill each with 1/4 cup chili mixture and cheese piece.

wing it!

Add color and flavor by putting strips of red, yellow or green bell pepper on top of cheese slices when making these stacks. Finish with a dollop of sour cream.

1 **SERVING:** Calories 240 (Calories from Fat 80); Fat 9g (Saturated 4g); Cholesterol 60mg; Sodium 600mg; Carbohydrate 28g (Dietary Fiber 3g); Protein 12g • % **DAILY VALUE:** Vitamin A 10%; Vitamin C 6%; Calcium 8%; Iron 12% • **DIET EXCHANGES:** 2 Starch, 1 Medium-Fat Meat • **CARBOHYDRATE CHOICES:** 2

prep: 20 min

wing it!

Chicken with fruits and vegetables gives you a hefty dose of vitamins, minerals and protein in one tasty combination. The mango adds color, a bit of sweetness and vitamin A to this dish.

4 SERVINGS

Chicken Salad in Pitas

2 pita breads (6 inches in diameter)

2 cups chopped cooked chicken

1 cup frozen green peas, thawed and drained

1/2 cup mayonnaise or salad dressing

1/4 teaspoon salt

1/4 teaspoon pepper

1 medium stalk celery, chopped (1/2 cup)

4 medium green onions, sliced (4 tablespoons)

1 small mango, peeled, pitted and diced (3/4 cup)

1 Cut pita breads in half; open to form pockets. Mix remaining ingredients.

2 Divide chicken mixture among pita bread halves.

1 SANDWICH: Calories 475 (Calories from Fat 245); Fat 27g (Saturated 5g); Cholesterol 75mg; Sodium 560mg; Carbohydrate 32g (Dietary Fiber 4g); Protein 25g • **% DAILY VALUE:** Vitamin A 14%; Vitamin C 34%; Calcium 6%; Iron 14% • **DIET EXCHANGES:** 2 Starch, 2 1/2 High-Fat Meat, 1 1/2 Fat • **CARBOHYDRATE CHOICES:** 2

Chicken Salad in Pitas

prep: **15 min**

wing it!

If you can't find garlic-and-herb seasoning, mix together 1/2 teaspoon dried basil leaves, 1/4 teaspoon dried thyme leaves, 1/4 teaspoon garlic powder and 1/8 teaspoon pepper.

4 SANDWICHES

Chicken Salad on Focaccia

3 cups chopped cooked chicken

3 medium stalks celery, finely chopped (1 1/2 cups)

1/2 cup mayonnaise or salad dressing

1 teaspoon garlic-and-herb seasoning

1 round focaccia bread (10 to 12 inches in diameter), cut horizontally in half

1 Mix chicken, celery, mayonnaise and seasoning.

2 Spread mixture over bottom half of focaccia bread; top with remaining half. Cut into wedges.

1 SANDWICH: Calories 675 (Calories from Fat 340); Fat 38g (Saturated 7g); Cholesterol 105mg; Sodium 1090mg; Carbohydrate 48g (Dietary Fiber 2g); Protein 36g • **% DAILY VALUE:** Vitamin A 2%; Vitamin C 2%; Calcium 4%; Iron 24% • **DIET EXCHANGES:** 3 Starch, 1 Vegetable, 3 1/2 Medium-Fat Meat, 3 Fat • **CARBOHYDRATE CHOICES: 3**

Chicken Salad on Focaccia

prep: 10 min
cook: 5 min

wing
it !

Instead of Italian
bread, try onion
or herb focaccia
for a change.
Slice the focaccia
horizontally in
half and spread
each cut side
with butter. Cut
focaccia into
4 wedges. Layer
chicken, pesto
and cheese on
bottom wedges
and place on
large cookie
sheet. Add tops
of wedges, cut
sides up, broil
4 to 6 inches
from heat for
3 minutes.

4 SANDWICHES

Chicken-Pesto Panini

8 slices Italian bread, 1/2 inch thick

2 tablespoons butter or margarine, softened

8 slices cooked chicken

4 tablespoons basil pesto

4 slices (1 ounce each) mozzarella cheese

Spaghetti sauce, warmed, if desired

1 Spread one side of each bread slice with butter. Place 4 bread slices butter sides down; top with chicken, pesto and cheese. Top with remaining bread slices, butter sides up.

2 Cover and cook sandwiches in 12-inch skillet over medium heat 4 to 5 minutes, turning once, until bread is crisp and cheese is melted. Serve with spaghetti sauce.

1 SANDWICH: Calories 435 (Calories from Fat 225); Fat 25g (Saturated 7g); Cholesterol 70mg; Sodium 635mg; Carbohydrate 22g (Dietary Fiber 1g); Protein 30g • % DAILY VALUE: Vitamin A 12%; Vitamin C 0%; Calcium 30%; Iron 12% • DIET EXCHANGES: 1 1/2 Starch, 4 Medium-Fat Meat • CARBOHYDRATE CHOICES: 1 1/2

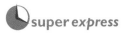

4 SERVINGS

Philly Chicken Panini

prep: 10 min
cook: 5 min

8 slices rye or pumpernickel bread, 1/2 inch thick

2 tablespoons butter or margarine, softened

8 slices cooked chicken

4 slices (1 ounce each) mozzarella cheese

1 Spread one side of each bread slice with butter. Place 4 bread slices butter sides down in 12-inch skillet; top with chicken and cheese. Top with remaining bread slices, butter sides up.

2 Cover and cook sandwiches over medium heat 4 to 5 minutes, turning once, until bread is crisp and cheese is melted.

wing it!

Now you can make this take-out favorite at home in just minutes. Make it Italian by adding basil, pesto and slices of tomatoes.

1 SANDWICH: Calories 365 (Calories from Fat 145); Fat 16g (Saturated 6g); Cholesterol 65mg; Sodium 610mg; Carbohydrate 26g (Dietary Fiber 3g); Protein 29g • % DAILY VALUE: Vitamin A 10%; Vitamin C 0%; Calcium 26%; Iron 12% • DIET EXCHANGES: 2 Starch, 3 Medium-Fat Meat • CARBOHYDRATE CHOICES: 2

prep: 15 min
bake: 16 min

Chicken Club Squares

wing it!

Love the flavor of BLTs? While this "sandwich" bakes, shred 1 1/2 cups of iceberg or romaine lettuce; toss a couple handfuls over each serving immediately after cutting into squares.

2 cups Original Bisquick mix

1/3 cup mayonnaise or salad dressing

1/3 cup milk

2 cups cubed cooked chicken

2 medium green onions, sliced (2 tablespoons)

4 slices bacon, crisply cooked and crumbled

1/4 cup mayonnaise or salad dressing

1 large tomato, chopped (1 cup)

1 cup shredded reduced-fat mozzarella cheese (4 ounces)

1 Heat oven to 450°. Grease cookie sheet with shortening or butter.

2 Stir Bisquick mix, 1/3 cup mayonnaise and the milk until soft dough forms. Roll or pat dough into 12 × 8-inch rectangle on cookie sheet. Bake 8 to 10 minutes or until golden brown.

3 Mix chicken, onions, bacon and 1/4 cup mayonnaise. Spread over crust to within 1/4 inch of edge. Sprinkle with tomato and cheese.

4 Bake 5 to 6 minutes or until chicken mixture is hot and cheese is melted. Cut into squares.

1 SERVING: Calories 490 (Calories from Fat 290); Fat 32g (Saturated 8g); Cholesterol 65mg; Sodium 910mg; Carbohydrate 28g (Dietary Fiber 1g); Protein 23g • % DAILY VALUE: Vitamin A 8%; Vitamin C 4%; Calcium 24%; Iron 12% • DIET EXCHANGES: 2 Starch, 2 1/2 Medium-Fat Meat, 3 Fat • CARBOHYDRATE CHOICES: 2

Calzone

prep: **45 min**
bake: **25 min**

1 can refrigerated pizza crust dough

2 cups shredded mozzarella cheese (8 ounces)

1 cup cooked chicken, cut into thin strips

1/2 cup ricotta cheese

1/4 cup chopped fresh basil leaves

2 roma (plum) tomatoes, chopped

Freshly ground pepper

1 large egg, slightly beaten

wingit!

A calzone is a stuffed pizza that looks like a big turnover. For extra flavor, serve with a jar of tomato sauce for dipping. That's the traditional way!

1 Heat oven to 375°. Grease 2 cookie sheets.

2 Divide dough into 6 equal parts. Roll each part into 7-inch circle on lightly floured surface with floured rolling pin.

3 Top half of each dough circle with mozzarella cheese, chicken, ricotta cheese, basil and tomatoes to within 1 inch of edge. Sprinkle with pepper. Carefully fold dough over filling; pinch edges or press with fork to seal securely.

4 Place calzones on cookie sheets. Brush with egg. Bake about 25 minutes or until golden brown.

1 SERVING: Calories 440 (Calories from Fat 155); Fat 17g (Saturated 7g); Cholesterol 100mg; Sodium 630mg; Carbohydrate 40g (Dietary Fiber 2g); Protein 32g • **% DAILY VALUE:** Vitamin A 14%; Vitamin C 4%; Calcium 34%; Iron 12% • **DIET EXCHANGES:** 2 1/2 Starch, 3 Medium-Fat Meat • **CARBOHYDRATE CHOICES:** 2 1/2

BBQ Chicken Pizza

3 packages (8 ounces each) Italian bread shells or 6 pita breads (6 inches in diameter)

3/4 cup barbecue sauce

1 1/2 cups cut-up cooked chicken

3/4 cup shredded smoked or regular Cheddar cheese (3 ounces)

6 tablespoons chopped red onion

1 Heat oven to 450°. Place bread shells on ungreased large cookie sheet.

2 Spread barbecue sauce on bread shells to within 1/4 inch of edges. Top with chicken and cheese. Sprinkle with onion. Bake 7 to 12 minutes or until cheese is melted.

wing it!

Purchased pizza crust, rotisserie chicken and shredded cheese make this one of the easiest pizzas you'll ever make. Add extra zest by sprinkling the pizza with 6 tablespoons of chopped red onion.

1 SERVING: Calories 330 (Calories from Fat 70); Fat 8g (Saturated 4g); Cholesterol 45mg; Sodium 750mg; Carbohydrate 45g (Dietary Fiber 2g); Protein 19g • % **DAILY VALUE:** Vitamin A 4%; Vitamin C 0%; Calcium 14%; Iron 12% • **DIET EXCHANGES:** 3 Starch, 1 1/2 Lean Meat • **CARBOHYDRATE CHOICES:** 3

BBQ Chicken Pizza

California Pizza

prep: **5 min**
bake: **25 min**

wing it!

Need some avocado advice? Choose avocados that are heavy for their size and don't have nicks or bruises. Store unripe avocados at room temperature and ripe ones in the refrigerator for up to a week. If you want to speed up the ripening process, place avocados in a paper bag and let them stand at room temperature for a couple of days.

I can (8 ounces) tomato sauce

I teaspoon dried oregano leaves

1/2 teaspoon dried basil leaves

1/2 teaspoon salt

1/4 teaspoon garlic or onion powder

1/8 teaspoon pepper

2 cups **Original Bisquick mix**

1/2 cup cold water

1 1/2 cups shredded Monterey Jack cheese (6 ounces)

2 cups cut-up cooked chicken

1/2 cup sliced ripe olives

I medium avocado, sliced

1 Heat oven to 425°. Grease 12-inch pizza pan. Mix tomato sauce, oregano, basil, salt, garlic powder and pepper; set aside.

2 Mix Bisquick mix and cold water until soft dough forms. Press dough in pizza pan, using fingers dusted with Bisquick mix; pinch edge to form 1/2-inch rim. Sprinkle 1/2 cup of the cheese over dough. Spread tomato sauce over cheese. Top with chicken and olives. Sprinkle with remaining 1 cup cheese.

3 Bake 20 to 25 minutes or until crust is golden brown and cheese is bubbly. Garnish with avocado slices.

1 SERVING: 320 (Calories from Fat 155); Fat 17g (Saturated 6g); Cholesterol 50mg; Sodium 980mg; Carbohydrate 23g (Dietary Fiber 2g); Protein 18g • % DAILY VALUE: Vitamin A 12%; Vitamin C 2%; Calcium 22%; Iron 12% • DIET EXCHANGES: 1 1/2 Starch, 2 Medium-Fat Meat, 1 Fat • CARBOHYDRATE CHOICES: 1 1/2

California Pizza

Chicken Enchilada Pizzas

prep: 15 min
bake: 6 min

4 flour tortillas (8 to 10 inches in diameter)

1 tablespoon vegetable oil

1 medium onion, thinly sliced

2 cups chopped cooked chicken

1/2 cup green salsa (salsa verde)

1 can (2 1/4 ounces) sliced ripe olives, drained

1/3 cup sour cream

1 cup shredded Monterey Jack cheese (4 ounces)

1 Heat oven to 400°. Place tortillas on ungreased cookie sheet. Bake about 5 minutes or until crisp.

2 While tortillas are baking, heat oil in 10-inch nonstick skillet over medium heat. Cook onion in oil, stirring frequently, until tender; remove from heat. Stir in chicken, salsa and olives.

3 Spread sour cream on tortillas. Top with chicken mixture and cheese. Bake 5 to 6 minutes, or until cheese is melted.

wing it!

As a quick addition, chop a large tomato and toss on this flavorful pizza between the chicken mixture and the cheese to add color and a fresh-from-the-garden flavor. Or after baking, sprinkle with chopped fresh cilantro.

1 SERVING: Calories 475 (Calories from Fat 225); Fat 25g (Saturated 11g); Cholesterol 100mg; Sodium 670mg; Carbohydrate 30g (Dietary Fiber 3g); Protein 32g • **% DAILY VALUE:** Vitamin A 14%; Vitamin C 4%; Calcium 32%; Iron 18% • **DIET EXCHANGES:** 2 Starch, 4 Medium-Fat Meat, 1/2 Fat • **CARBOHYDRATE CHOICES:** 2

4 SERVINGS

Chicken, Artichoke and Red Onion Pizza

prep: 10 min
bake: 10 min

2 teaspoons butter or margarine

1 large red onion, sliced (2 cups)

1 package (16 ounces) Italian bread shell or ready-to-serve pizza crust (12 to 14 inches in diameter)

1 cup cubed cooked chicken

1 jar (6 to 7 ounces) marinated artichoke hearts, drained and sliced

3 tablespoons sliced drained roasted red bell peppers (from 7-ounce jar)

1 cup shredded sharp Cheddar cheese (4 ounces)

1 Heat oven to 400°. Melt butter in 8-inch skillet over medium heat. Cook onion in butter 3 to 5 minutes, stirring occasionally, until crisp-tender.

2 Spread onion over bread shell. Top with chicken, artichoke hearts, bell peppers and cheese.

3 Bake 8 to 10 minutes or until cheese is melted.

wingit!

Artichoke hearts add a distinctive flavor to this easy pizza. Serve the pizza for a light supper, or cut into small squares for a great appetizer. If roasted red bell peppers aren't available, use canned pimientos.

1 SERVING: Calories 535 (Calories from Fat 200); Fat 22g (Saturated 11g); Cholesterol 75mg; Sodium 920mg; Carbohydrate 58g (Dietary Fiber 5g); Protein 31g • % DAILY VALUE: Vitamin A 22%; Vitamin C 16%; Calcium 18%; Iron 24% • DIET EXCHANGES: 3 Starch, 2 Vegetable, 2 1/2 High-Fat Meat • CARBOHYDRATE CHOICES: 4

prep: 10 min
bake: 12 min

wing it!

At your next party, cut thin slices of this chicken- and olive-laden pizza to serve as appetizers.

6 SERVINGS

Chicken–French Bread Pizza

- **1 loaf (1 pound) unsliced French bread**
- **1 can (8 ounces) pizza sauce**
- **2 cups cubed cooked chicken**
- **1 can (2 1/4 ounces) sliced ripe olives, drained**
- **1 cup shredded reduced-fat mozzarella cheese (4 ounces)**

1 Heat oven to 425°. Split bread horizontally in half. Place bread, cut sides up, on cookie sheet.

2 Spread pizza sauce over bread. Top with chicken and olives. Sprinkle with cheese. Bake about 12 minutes or until cheese is melted and chicken is heated through.

1 SERVING: Calories 375 (Calories from Fat 110); Fat 12g (Saturated 4g); Cholesterol 50mg; Sodium 820mg; Carbohydrate 42g (Dietary Fiber 3g); Protein 25g • % DAILY VALUE: Vitamin A 6%; Vitamin C 6%; Calcium 22%; Iron 18% • DIET EXCHANGES: 3 Starch, 2 Medium-Fat Meat • CARBOHYDRATE CHOICES: 3

Chicken–French Bread Pizza

wing it!

This is one of the easiest pizzas you'll ever make with purchased pizza crust, shredded cheese, spinach, and rotisserie chicken. It's a refreshing change of pace from the ordinary.

6 SERVINGS

Double-Cheese, Spinach and Chicken Pizza

I ready-to-serve pizza crust (12 to 14 inches in diameter)

I cup shredded Havarti cheese (4 ounces)

2 cups bagged washed fresh baby spinach leaves

I cup diced cooked chicken

1/4 cup chopped drained roasted red bell peppers (from 7-ounce jar)

1/2 teaspoon garlic salt

I cup shredded Cheddar cheese (4 ounces)

1 Heat oven to 425°. Place pizza crust on ungreased pizza pan.

2 Top with Havarti cheese, spinach, chicken, bell peppers, garlic salt and Cheddar cheese.

3 Bake 8 to 10 minutes or until crust is golden brown.

1 SERVING: Calories 580 (Calories from Fat 180); Fat 20g (Saturated 10g); Cholesterol 60mg; Sodium 970mg; Carbohydrate 72g (Dietary Fiber 5g); Protein 28g • **% DAILY VALUE:** Vitamin A 100%; Vitamin C 32%; Calcium 32%; Iron 40% • **DIET EXCHANGES:** 4 Starch, 2 Vegetable, 2 Medium-Fat Meat, 1 Fat • **CARBOHYDRATE CHOICES:** 5

Double-Cheese, Spinach and Chicken Pizza

Chicken Gyro Pizza

prep: 20 min
bake: 25 min

2 cups Original Bisquick mix

1/4 teaspoon dried oregano leaves

1/2 cup cold water

6 slices chicken breast, cut into strips

1 can (2 1/4 ounces) sliced ripe olives, drained

1/2 cup crumbled feta cheese (2 ounces)

1 1/2 cups shredded mozzarella cheese (6 ounces)

1 small tomato, chopped (1/2 cup)

1/2 cup chopped cucumber

1 Move oven rack to lowest position. Heat oven to 425°. Spray 12-inch pizza pan with cooking spray. Stir Bisquick mix, oregano and water; beat vigorously with spoon 20 strokes until soft dough forms. Press dough in pizza pan, using fingers dipped in Bisquick mix; pinch edge to form 1/2-inch rim. Bake about 15 minutes or until golden brown.

2 Top crust with chicken and olives; sprinkle with feta and mozzarella cheeses.

3 Bake about 10 minutes or until cheese is melted. Sprinkle with tomato and cucumber.

wing it!

The Mediterranean flavors and ingredients typical of a gyro—roasted meat with grilled vegetables and cucumber-yogurt sauce, rolled in pita bread—are transformed into a pizza the whole family will enjoy. If you prefer, mint leaves can be used in place of the oregano.

1 SERVING: Calories 310 (Calories from Fat 125); Fat 14g (Saturated 6g); Cholesterol 40mg; Sodium 910mg; Carbohydrate 27g (Dietary Fiber 1g); Protein 18g • % DAILY VALUE: Vitamin A 8%; Vitamin C 2%; Calcium 34%; Iron 10% • DIET EXCHANGES: 2 Starch, 2 Medium-Fat Meat • CARBOHYDRATE CHOICES: 2

Chicken Gyro Pizza

Chicken-Pesto Pizza

wing it!

For a lower-fat version, try reduced-fat pesto and sun-dried tomatoes that aren't packed in oil. Soak the sun-dried tomatoes as directed on package and then cut into slices.

1 package (16 ounces) Italian bread shell or ready-to-serve pizza crust (12 to 14 inches in diameter)

1 container (7 ounces) refrigerated basil pesto

1 cup chopped cooked chicken

4 roma (plum) tomatoes, chopped

1/4 cup oil-packed sun-dried tomatoes, drained and sliced

1 1/2 cups shredded provolone cheese (6 ounces)

1 Heat oven to 450°. Place bread shell on ungreased cookie sheet.

2 Spread pesto evenly over bread shell. Top with chicken, tomatoes and cheese. Bake about 10 minutes or until cheese is melted.

1 SERVING: Calories 825 (Calories from Fat 430); Fat 48g (Saturated 17g); Cholesterol 80mg; Sodium 1450mg; Carbohydrate 60g (Dietary Fiber 5g); Protein 39g • % DAILY VALUE: Vitamin A 34%; Vitamin C 22%; Calcium 54%; Iron 32% • DIET EXCHANGES: 3 1/2 Starch, 1 Vegetable, 3 Medium-Fat Meat, 6 1/2 Fat • CARBOHYDRATE CHOICES: 4

Chicken-Pesto Pizza

prep: 10 min
bake: 10 min

wing it!

The great escape! You're off to Hawaii when you serve up this pizza. Can't find pineapple tidbits? Crushed pineapple, very well drained, can be used instead.

6 SERVINGS

Hawaiian Pizza

I Italian bread shell or ready-to-serve pizza crust (12 inches in diameter)

I can (8 ounces) tomato sauce

2 cups cubed cooked chicken

I can (8 ounces) pineapple tidbits, well drained

I cup shredded mozzarella cheese (4 ounces)

1 Heat oven to 400°. Place bread shell on ungreased cookie sheet.

2 Spread tomato sauce over bread shell. Top with chicken and pineapple. Sprinkle with cheese. Bake 8 to 10 minutes or until pizza is hot and cheese is melted.

1 SERVING: Calories 370 (Calories from Fat 100); Fat 11g (Saturated 5g); Cholesterol 60mg; Sodium 760mg; Carbohydrate 41g (Dietary Fiber 2g); Protein 27g • **% DAILY VALUE:** Vitamin A 10%; Vitamin C 6%; Calcium 16%; Iron 16% • **DIET EXCHANGES:** 2 Starch, 1/2 Fruit, 2 1/2 Medium-Fat Meat • **CARBOHYDRATE CHOICES:** 3

Hawaiian Pizza

Mini White Pizzas

prep: **20 min**
bake: **11 min**

wing it!

Using boiling water makes the pizza dough more chewy and flavorful. Keep it to one step by measuring 1/3 cup water in a small glass measuring cup and microwaving on High until full bubbles appear.

1 1/2 cups Original Bisquick mix

1/3 cup boiling water

1/2 cup reduced-fat or regular Alfredo sauce

1/2 cup finely chopped cooked chicken

1/2 cup chopped fresh mushrooms

2 tablespoons chopped fresh or 1 teaspoon dried basil leaves

1 cup shredded mozzarella cheese (4 ounces)

Additional fresh basil leaves, if desired

1 Heat oven to 450°. Spray large cookie sheet with cooking spray. Stir Bisquick mix and water until soft dough forms. Divide dough into fourths. Pat each part of dough into 6-inch circle on cookie sheet, using fingers dusted with Bisquick mix; pinch edge to form 1/2-inch rim.

2 Spread Alfredo sauce on dough. Top with chicken, mushrooms and chopped basil. Sprinkle with cheese.

3 Bake 9 to 11 minutes or until crusts are golden brown and cheese is bubbly. Garnish with additional basil leaves.

1 PIZZA: Calories 340 (Calories from Fat 145); Fat 16g (Saturated 7g); Cholesterol 40mg; Sodium 940mg; Carbohydrate 31g (Dietary Fiber 1g); Protein 18g • **% DAILY VALUE:** Vitamin A 8%; Vitamin C 0%; Calcium 34%; Iron 10% • **DIET EXCHANGES:** 2 Starch, 2 Medium-Fat Meat, 1 Fat • **CARBOHYDRATE CHOICES:** 2

Mini White Pizzas

Thai Chicken Pizzas

prep: 10 min
bake: 20 min

wing it!

For added speed, you can use slightly less than 1 cup of purchased peanut sauce, found in the Asian foods section of most supermarkets, in place of the peanut butter, soy sauce, vinegar and sugar.

6 flour tortillas (8 to 10 inches in diameter)

1/2 cup peanut butter

1/4 cup soy sauce

2 tablespoons seasoned rice vinegar

2 teaspoons sugar

2 cups shredded mozzarella cheese (8 ounces)

2 cups chopped cooked chicken

1 bag (1 pound) frozen stir-fry vegetables, thawed and drained

1 Heat oven to 400°. Place tortillas on ungreased cookie sheet. Bake about 5 minutes or until crisp.

2 Mix peanut butter, soy sauce, vinegar and sugar; spread over tortillas. Top each with 1/4 cup of the cheese. Spread chicken and vegetables evenly over tortillas. Sprinkle with remaining 1/2 cup cheese.

3 Bake 10 to 15 minutes or until pizzas are hot and cheese is melted.

1 SERVING: Calories 490 (Calories from Fat 215); Fat 24g (Saturated 8g); Cholesterol 60mg; Sodium 1340mg; Carbohydrate 37g (Dietary Fiber 5g); Protein 36g • % DAILY VALUE: Vitamin A 20%; Vitamin C 20%; Calcium 36%; Iron 18% • DIET EXCHANGES: 2 Starch, 1 Vegetable, 4 Lean Meat, 2 Fat • CARBOHYDRATE CHOICES: 2 1/2

5 Pastas in Moments

prep: **10 min**
cook: **15 min**

wing it!

If you like olives, add some sliced olives with the chicken. Make the meal complete by serving with a loaf of Italian bread and extra-virgin olive oil for dipping and fresh sliced tomatoes.

Bow-Ties with Chicken, Pesto and Roasted Red Peppers

3 cups uncooked farfalle (bow-tie) pasta (6 ounces)

2 cups cubed cooked chicken

1/2 cup basil pesto

1/2 cup coarsely chopped roasted red bell peppers (from 7-ounce jar)

1 Cook pasta in 3-quart saucepan as directed on package; drain. Return pasta to saucepan.

2 Add chicken, pesto and bell peppers to pasta. Heat over low heat about 15 minutes, stirring constantly, until hot.

1 SERVING: Calories 455 (Calories from Fat 200); Fat 22g (Saturated 5g); Cholesterol 65mg; Sodium 550mg; Carbohydrate 36g (Dietary Fiber 3g); Protein 28g • **% DAILY VALUE:** Vitamin A 30%; Vitamin C 34%; Calcium 14%; Iron 18% • **DIET EXCHANGES:** 2 1/2 Starch, 3 Medium-Fat Meat, 1/2 Fat • **CARBOHYDRATE CHOICES:** 2 1/2

Bow-Ties with Chicken, Pesto and Roasted Red Peppers

Golden-Crusted Chicken-Asparagus Lasagna

prep: **35 min**
bake: **45 min**
stand: **10 min**

wing it!

The whipping cream and cheese mixture that top this recipe form a pretty, golden brown, crispy topping. To "whip" up this topping in a flash, make sure that your cream is as cold as possible and chill the beaters and bowl for a few minutes in the freezer.

9 uncooked lasagna noodles (9 ounces)

2 pounds asparagus, cut into 2-inch pieces

1 tablespoon olive or vegetable oil

1/2 teaspoon lemon pepper seasoning salt

3 tablespoons butter or margarine

1/4 cup all-purpose flour

1 can (14 1/2 ounces) ready-to-serve chicken broth

1/2 cup milk

2 teaspoons chopped fresh or 1/2 teaspoon dried marjoram leaves

2 cups diced cooked chicken

1/2 cup roasted red bell peppers (from 7-ounce jar), drained and chopped

3/4 cup shredded Parmesan cheese

2 cups shredded mozzarella cheese (8 ounces)

1/2 cup whipping (heavy) cream

1 Heat oven to 350°. Grease rectangular baking dish, 13 × 9 × 2 inches. Cook and drain noodles as directed on package.

2 Heat 5 cups water to boiling in 3-quart saucepan. Add asparagus; heat to boiling. Boil 3 to 4 minutes or until crisp-tender; drain. Place asparagus in bowl. Toss with oil and lemon pepper seasoning salt.

3 Melt butter in 2-quart saucepan over medium heat. Stir in flour. Cook 1 minute, stirring constantly. Stir in broth, milk and marjoram. Heat to boiling, stirring constantly. Stir in chicken, 1/4 cup of the bell peppers and 1/2 cup of the Parmesan cheese. Cook about 2 minutes or until hot.

4 Spread about 1/2 cup of the chicken mixture in baking dish. Top with 3 noodles, 1 1/2 cups chicken mixture, half of the asparagus and 1 cup of the mozzarella cheese. Repeat layers, starting with noodles. Top with remaining 3 noodles.

5 Beat whipping cream in chilled small bowl with electric mixer on high speed until stiff peaks form. Spread over top of lasagna. Sprinkle with remaining 1/4 cup bell peppers and 1/4 cup Parmesan cheese. Bake uncovered 40 to 45 minutes or until hot in center and top is golden brown. Let stand 10 minutes before cutting.

1 **SERVING:** Calories 455 (Calories from Fat 200); Fat 22g (Saturated 10g); Cholesterol 70mg; Sodium 870mg; Carbohydrate 34g (Dietary Fiber 2g); Protein 30g • % **DAILY VALUE:** Vitamin A 36%; Vitamin C 28%; Calcium 40%; Iron 14% • **DIET EXCHANGES:** 2 Starch, 1 Vegetable, 3 Medium-Fat Meat, 1 Fat • **CARBOHYDRATE CHOICES:** 2

Golden-Crusted Chicken-Asparagus Lasagna

Chicken Enchilada Lasagna Bundles

prep: **35 min**
bake: **45 min**

wing it!

Pass around bowls of salsa and extra sour cream, so your guests can help themselves. For an extra-special touch, stir 1 teaspoon lime juice into 1 cup sour cream and sprinkle with grated lime peel.

12 uncooked lasagna noodles (12 ounces)

2 cans (10 ounces each) enchilada sauce

1 can (4 1/2 ounces) chopped green chiles

1 medium tomato, chopped (3/4 cup)

2 cups diced cooked chicken

1 cup shredded Monterey Jack cheese with jalapeño chiles (4 ounces)

8 medium green onions, chopped (1/2 cup)

1 cup sour cream

1 cup shredded Cheddar cheese (4 ounces)

Sour cream, if desired

Shredded lettuce, if desired

1 Heat oven to 350°. Grease rectangular baking dish, 13 × 9 × 2 inches. Cook and drain noodles as directed on package.

2 Mix enchilada sauce, chiles and tomato. Mix chicken, Monterey Jack cheese, onions and 1 cup sour cream.

3 Spread about 1/2 cup sauce mixture in baking dish. Spread about 1 teaspoon sauce mixture over each noodle; spread evenly with about 1/4 cup of the chicken mixture. Roll up each noodle; place seam side down on sauce in dish. Spoon about 1 cup sauce mixture over rolls. Sprinkle with Cheddar cheese.

4 Cover and bake 40 to 45 minutes or until hot in center. Heat remaining sauce mixture in 1 1/2-quart saucepan; spoon over rolls. Top with sour cream and lettuce.

1 SERVING: Calories 505 (Calories from Fat 215); Fat 24g (Saturated 13g); Cholesterol 100mg; Sodium 1160mg; Carbohydrate 42g (Dietary Fiber 4g); Protein 31g • **% DAILY VALUE:** Vitamin A 36%; Vitamin C 18%; Calcium 34%; Iron 22% • **DIET EXCHANGES:** 3 Starch, 3 Medium-Fat Meat, 1 Fat • **CARBOHYDRATE CHOICES:** 3

Chicken Enchilada Lasagna Bundles

Chicken Lasagna with Tarragon-Cheese Sauce

prep: **35 min**
bake: **30 min**
stand: **10 min**

wing it!

A flexible plastic spatula is ideal for serving lasagna. You'll be able to dig underneath each piece, so that nobody is cheated out of any cheese, sauce or noodles.

6 uncooked lasagna noodles (6 ounces)

1 tablespoon butter or margarine

1 1/2 cups sliced mushrooms (4 ounces)

1 medium onion, chopped (1/2 cup)

1 cup ready-to-serve chicken broth

2 tablespoons chopped fresh or 1 teaspoon dried tarragon leaves

1/4 teaspoon salt

1/4 teaspoon pepper

1 package (8 ounces) cream cheese, softened

1 cup shredded Swiss cheese (4 ounces)

1 1/2 cups diced cooked chicken

1 jar (2 ounces) diced pimientos, drained

1 Heat oven to 325°. Grease rectangular baking dish, 11 × 7 × 1 1/2 inches. Cook and drain noodles as directed on package.

2 Melt butter in 12-inch skillet over medium heat. Cook mushrooms and onion in butter, stirring occasionally, until tender. Stir in broth, 1 tablespoon of the tarragon, the salt and pepper. Heat to boiling; reduce heat to low. Stir in cream cheese and Swiss cheese until melted. Stir in chicken and pimientos.

3 Cut noodles crosswise in half. Arrange 6 pieces, overlapping edges, in baking dish. Spread half of the sauce over noodles. Repeat layers of noodles and sauce. Cover and bake 25 to 30 minutes or until hot in center and bubbly around edges. Sprinkle with remaining 1 tablespoon tarragon. Let stand 10 minutes before cutting.

1 **SERVING:** Calories 385 (Calories from Fat 215); Fat 24g (Saturated 13g); Cholesterol 90mg; Sodium 560mg; Carbohydrate 20g (Dietary Fiber 1g); Protein 22g • % **DAILY VALUE:** Vitamin A 20%; Vitamin C 6%; Calcium 22%; Iron 12% • **DIET EXCHANGES:** 1 Starch, 3 High-Fat Meat • **CARBOHYDRATE CHOICES:** 1

Chicken Spaghetti Olé

prep: 30 min
bake: 30 min

6 ounces uncooked spaghetti

1 tablespoon butter or margarine

1 small green bell pepper, chopped (1/2 cup)

1 medium stalk celery, chopped (1/2 cup)

1 small onion, chopped (1/4 cup)

1 can (10 ounces) diced tomatoes and green chiles, undrained

1 can (8 ounces) tomato sauce

1 package (8 ounces) process cheese spread loaf, cut into cubes

1/2 teaspoon salt

1/4 teaspoon pepper

2 cups diced cooked chicken

Sliced jalepeño chiles, if desired

1 Heat oven to 350°. Spray rectangular baking dish, $13 \times 9 \times 2$ inches, with cooking spray. Cook and drain spaghetti as directed on package.

2 While spaghetti is cooking, melt butter in 12-inch skillet over medium heat. Cook bell pepper, celery and onion in butter, stirring occasionally, until tender. Stir in tomatoes, tomato sauce, cheese, salt and pepper; reduce heat to low. Heat, stirring frequently, until cheese is melted.

3 Stir in chicken and spaghetti. Spoon into baking dish. Bake uncovered about 30 minutes or until bubbly around edges. Top with chiles.

wing it!

Give your family a tasty reminder of summer by serving corn on the cob and sliced cucumbers in the middle of the winter. You'll find packaged ready-to-cook fresh ears of corn in the produce or freezer section of your super-market, and cucumbers are available in the produce section all year-round. What a fresh treat!

1 SERVING: Calories 380 (Calories from Fat 160); Fat 18g (Saturated10g); Cholesterol 805mg; Sodium 1265mg; Carbohydrate 32g (Dietary Fiber 3g); Protein 26g • % DAILY VALUE: Vitamin A 20%; Vitamin C 18%; Calcium 22%; Iron 14% • DIET EXCHANGES: 2 Starch, 3 Medium-Fat Meat • CARBOHYDRATE CHOICES: 2

Chicken Tetrazzini

prep: 25 min
bake: 30 min

wing it!

This rich casserole apparently got its name from the opera singer Luisa Tetrazzini. To complete this delicious meal, all you need to add is a tossed salad with an Italian dressing.

1 package (7 ounces) spaghetti, broken into thirds

1/4 cup butter or margarine

1/4 cup all-purpose flour

1/2 teaspoon salt

1/4 teaspoon pepper

1 cup ready-to-serve chicken broth

1 cup whipping (heavy) cream

2 tablespoons sherry or water

2 cups cubed cooked chicken

1 can (4 ounces) sliced mushrooms, drained

1/2 cup grated Parmesan cheese

1 Heat oven to 350°. Cook and drain spaghetti as directed on package.

2 Melt butter in 2-quart saucepan over low heat. Stir flour, salt and pepper into butter. Cook over medium heat, stirring constantly, until mixture is smooth and bubbly; remove from heat. Gradually stir in broth and whipping cream. Heat to boiling, stirring constantly. Boil and stir 1 minute. Stir in sherry, spaghetti, chicken and mushrooms.

3 Pour spaghetti mixture into ungreased 2-quart casserole. Sprinkle with cheese. Bake uncovered about 30 minutes or until bubbly in center.

1 SERVING: Calories 465 (Calories from Fat 245); Fat 27g (Saturated 12g); Cholesterol 90mg; Sodium 860mg; Carbohydrate 33g (Dietary Fiber 2g); Protein 23g • % DAILY VALUE: Vitamin A 20%; Vitamin C 0%; Calcium 16%; Iron 14% • DIET EXCHANGES: 2 Starch, 2 1/2 Medium-Fat Meat, 2 1/2 Fat • CARBOHYDRATE CHOICES: 2

Chicken Tetrazzini

Chicken and Ham Tetrazzini

prep: 15 min
bake: 35 min

wing it!

Get creative!
Food arranged in
artistic patterns
is a joy to eat.
It looks as good
as it tastes!
Arrange a platter
of sliced fruits
and vegetables
with cucumber,
zucchini or green
bell peppers on
the outside and
grape or cherry
tomatoes and
baby carrots on
the inside.

1 package (9 ounces) refrigerated linguine

1 can (10 3/4 ounces) condensed cream of mushroom soup

1 can (10 3/4 ounces) condensed cream of chicken soup

3/4 cup milk

2 tablespoons dry white wine or apple juice

2 cups cut-up cooked chicken

1/2 cup cut-up fully cooked smoked ham

1 small green bell pepper, chopped (1/2 cup)

1/4 cup sliced pitted ripe olives

1/2 cup grated Parmesan cheese

1/4 cup slivered almonds, toasted

1 Heat oven to 375°. Cook and drain linguine as directed on package.

2 While linguine is cooking, mix soups, milk and wine in ungreased 2-quart casserole. Stir in linguine, chicken, ham, bell pepper and olives. Sprinkle with cheese.

3 Bake uncovered about 35 minutes or until hot and bubbly. Sprinkle with almonds.

1 SERVING: Calories 455 (Calories from Fat 155); Fat 17g (Saturated 5g); Cholesterol 60mg; Sodium 1310mg; Carbohydrate 46g (Dietary Fiber 3g); Protein 29g • % DAILY VALUE: Vitamin A 8%; Vitamin C 8%; Calcium 20%; Iron 18% • DIET EXCHANGES: 3 Starch, 3 Medium-Fat Meat • CARBOHYDRATE CHOICES: 3

Creamy Chicken and Corn with Fettuccine

prep: 15 min
cook: 8 min

8 ounces uncooked fettuccine or linguine

1 package (10 ounces) frozen whole kernel corn, thawed

6 medium green onions, sliced (6 tablespoons)

1 tub (8 ounces) roasted-garlic reduced-fat cream cheese

1/3 cup skim milk

1 1/2 cups cut-up cooked chicken

1 jar (2 ounces) diced pimientos, drained

1/4 teaspoon pepper

Chopped fresh parsley, if desired

wing it!

If you'd like to reduce the fat in this recipe even more, substitute fat-free cream cheese with garden vegetables for the reduced-fat roasted-garlic version.

1 Cook fettuccine as directed on package.

2 While fettuccine is cooking, spray 12-inch nonstick skillet with cooking spray; heat over medium heat. Cook corn and onions in skillet about 4 minutes, stirring frequently, until corn is crisp-tender.

3 Stir cream cheese and milk into corn mixture until blended. Stir in chicken, pimientos and pepper; heat through.

4 Drain fettuccine. Stir fettuccine into cheese sauce mixture; heat through. Sprinkle with parsley.

1 SERVING: Calories 565 (Calories from Fat 215); Fat 24g (Saturated 12g); Cholesterol 145mg; Sodium 450mg; Carbohydrate 60g (Dietary Fiber 4g); Protein 28g • % DAILY VALUE: Vitamin A 26%; Vitamin C 12%; Calcium 10%; Iron 24% • DIET EXCHANGES: 4 Starch, 2 Medium-Fat Meat, 1/2 Fat • CARBOHYDRATE CHOICES: 4

Chicken and Fettuccine

prep: 15 min
cook: 18 min

wing it!

Add more color to this tasty pasta dish by using tomato-basil, spinach or herb pasta.

8 ounces uncooked fettuccine	**1 teaspoon garlic salt**
3 cups chopped cooked chicken	**2 large tomatoes, chopped (2 cups)**
3 tablespoons olive or vegetable oil	**Chopped fresh basil leaves, if desired**

1 Cook and drain pasta as directed on package.

2 Toss pasta and remaining ingredients except basil. Top with basil.

1 SERVING: Calories 335 (Calories from Fat 125); Fat 13g (Saturated 3g); Cholesterol 95mg; Sodium 390mg; Carbohydrate 27g (Dietary Fiber 2g); Protein 25g • % DAILY VALUE: Vitamin A 10%; Vitamin C 10%; Calcium 2%; Iron 14% • DIET EXCHANGES: 1 1/2 Starch, 1 Vegetable, 2 1/2 Medium-Fat Meat • CARBOHYDRATE CHOICES: 2

Spinach Fettuccine Casserole with Chicken and Bacon

prep: **25 min**
bake: **30 min**

1 package (9 ounces) refrigerated spinach fettuccine

3 tablespoons butter or margarine

3 tablespoons all-purpose flour

1 can (14 1/2 ounces) ready-to-serve chicken broth

1/2 cup half-and-half

1 1/2 cups cubed cooked chicken

1/2 cup oil-packed sun-dried tomatoes, drained and cut into thin strips

2 slices bacon, crisply cooked and crumbled

3 tablespoons shredded Parmesan cheese

wing it!

This casserole is sure to be a crowd-pleasing winner! The recipe can easily be doubled and baked in a 13 × 9 × 2-inch baking dish.

1 Heat oven to 350°. Spray square baking dish, 8 × 8 × 2 inches, with cooking spray. Cook and drain fettuccine as directed on package.

2 Melt butter in 2-quart saucepan over medium heat. Stir in flour. Gradually stir in broth. Heat to boiling, stirring constantly; remove from heat. Stir in half-and-half.

3 Stir in chicken, tomatoes and bacon. Add fettuccine; toss gently to mix well. Spoon into baking dish. Sprinkle with cheese. Bake uncovered about 30 minutes or until hot in center.

1 SERVING: Calories 540 (Calories from Fat 215); Fat 24g (Saturated 7g); Cholesterol 120mg; Sodium 1040mg; Carbohydrate 51g (Dietary Fiber 3g); Protein 30g • % DAILY VALUE: Vitamin A 18%; Vitamin C 12%; Calcium 14%; Iron 24% • DIET EXCHANGES: 3 Starch, 1 Vegetable, 3 Medium-Fat Meat, 1 Fat • CARBOHYDRATE CHOICES: 3 1/2

Greek Orzo Chicken

prep: 25 min

4 cups cooked orzo or rosamarina pasta

1 cup shredded cooked chicken

2 medium cucumbers, chopped (1 1/2 cups)

1 medium red or green bell pepper, chopped (1 cup)

1/3 cup balsamic vinaigrette

1/2 cup pitted Kalamata or Greek olives

1/4 cup crumbled feta cheese

1 Place pasta, chicken, cucumbers and bell pepper in large bowl.

2 Pour vinaigrette over salad; toss until coated. Top with olives and cheese.

wing it!

Kalamata olives, grown in the Mediterranean, are sun ripened, cured and pickled in brine. Available both pitted and unpitted, they have a salty, mild wine flavor and a texture that is soft and creamy.

1 SERVING: Calories 405 (Calories from Fat 145); Fat 16g (Saturated 3g); Cholesterol 40mg; Sodium 670mg; Carbohydrate 46g (Dietary Fiber 3g); Protein 19g • % DAILY VALUE: Vitamin A 38%; Vitamin C 48%; Calcium 10%; Iron 18% • DIET EXCHANGES: 2 1/2 Starch, 2 Vegetable, 1 Medium-Fat Meat, 2 Fat • CARBOHYDRATE CHOICES: 3

Greek Orzo Chicken

Pesto, Chicken and Pasta

prep: **10 min**
cook: **12 min**

wing it!

Look for reduced-fat pesto if you would like to shave some fat grams from this recipe. Another way to cut back on the fat in pesto is to skim off some of the oil that rises to the top of regular pesto.

3 cups uncooked farfalle (bow-tie) pasta (6 ounces)

2 cups cubed cooked chicken

1/2 cup pesto

1/2 cup coarsely chopped drained roasted red bell peppers (from 7-ounce jar)

Sliced ripe olives, if desired

1 Cook and drain pasta as directed on package, using 3-quart saucepan.

2 Mix hot cooked pasta, chicken, pesto and bell peppers in same saucepan. Heat over low heat, stirring constantly, until hot. Garnish with olives.

1 SERVING: Calories 455 (Calories from Fat 200); Fat 22g (Saturated 5g); Cholesterol 65mg; Sodium 550mg; Carbohydrate 36g (Dietary Fiber 3g); Protein 28g • % **DAILY VALUE:** Vitamin A 24%; Vitamin C 24%; Calcium 14%; Iron 18% • **DIET EXCHANGES:** 2 1/2 Starch, 3 Medium Fat-Meat, 1/2 Fat • **CARBOHYDRATE CHOICES:** 2 1/2

Pesto, Chicken and Pasta

Santa Fe Chicken-Tortellini Casserole

prep: **20 min**
bake: **35 min**

wing it!

Broken chips at the bottom of the chip bag are perfect for topping off this casserole. You also can place whole chips in a resealable plastic bag and crush them with a rolling pin.

1 package (9 ounces) refrigerated cheese-filled tortellini

3 tablespoons olive or vegetable oil

2 cups broccoli flowerets

1 medium onion, chopped (1/2 cup)

1 medium red bell pepper, chopped (1 cup)

3 tablespoons all-purpose flour

3/4 cup milk

3/4 cup ready-to-serve chicken broth

1 teaspoon ground cumin

4 cups cut-up cooked chicken

3/4 cup shredded Monterey Jack cheese (3 ounces)

1/2 cup shredded Colby cheese (2 ounces)

1/2 cup crushed tortilla chips

1 Heat oven to 325°. Grease 3-quart casserole. Cook and drain tortellini as directed on package. Heat 1 tablespoon of the oil in 10-inch skillet over medium-high heat. Cook broccoli, onion and bell pepper in oil about 3 minutes, stirring frequently, until crisp-tender. Remove broccoli mixture from skillet.

2 Cook flour and remaining 2 tablespoons oil in same skillet over low heat, stirring constantly, until smooth. Stir in milk, broth and cumin. Heat to boiling over medium heat, stirring constantly; remove from heat. Stir in chicken, Monterey Jack cheese, tortellini and broccoli mixture. Spoon into casserole.

3 Bake uncovered 25 to 35 minutes or until hot in center. During last several minutes of baking, sprinkle with Colby cheese and tortilla chips; bake until cheese is melted.

1 SERVING: Calories 485 (Calories from Fat 245); Fat 27g (Saturated 9g); Cholesterol 140mg; Sodium 430mg; Carbohydrate 21g (Dietary Fiber 2g); Protein 39g • % DAILY VALUE: Vitamin A 40%; Vitamin C 54%; Calcium 28%; Iron 16% • DIET EXCHANGES: 1 Starch, 1 Vegetable, 5 Medium-Fat Meat • CARBOHYDRATE CHOICES: 1 1/2

Santa Fe Chicken-Tortellini Casserole

Chicken and Pasta Stir-Fry

prep: 15 min
cook: 14 min

wing it!

If you'd like to serve six, this is an easy recipe to stretch. Add more veggies, like broccoli flowerets or sliced carrots, and more pasta, too. For interest, use a different shape or color of pasta.

2 cups uncooked farfalle (bow-tie) pasta (4 ounces)	**3 tablespoons chopped fresh or 1 tablespoon dried basil leaves**
1 pound asparagus, cut into 2-inch pieces (3 cups)	**3 tablespoons chopped sun-dried tomatoes (not oil-packed)**
2 medium onions, sliced	**1/4 teaspoon pepper**
1 1/2 cups ready-to-serve chicken broth	**Freshly grated Parmesan cheese, if desired**
2 cups cubed chicken	

1 Cook and drain pasta as directed on package.

2 Spray 12-inch skillet with cooking spray; heat over medium heat. Cook asparagus, onions and 1 cup of the broth in skillet 5 to 7 minutes, stirring occasionally, until liquid has evaporated.

3 Add chicken; stir-fry about 5 minutes to heat through.

4 Stir in remaining 1/2 cup broth, the basil, tomatoes, pepper and pasta. Cook about 2 minutes, stirring frequently, until mixture is hot. Sprinkle with cheese.

1 SERVING: Calories 380 (Calories from Fat 90); Fat 10g (Saturated 3g); Cholesterol 100mg; Sodium 650mg; Carbohydrate 31g (Dietary Fiber 3g); Protein 41g • % DAILY VALUE: Vitamin A 16%; Vitamin C 14%; Calcium 6%; Iron 18% • DIET EXCHANGES: 1 1/2 Starch, 1 Vegetable, 6 Very Lean Meat, 1/2 Fat • CARBOHYDRATE CHOICES: 2

6 Snappy Casseroles

Chicken Pot Pie

prep: **20 min**
bake: **40 min**
stand: **5 min**

wing it!

Serve this hearty pie with a bag of Caesar salad mix. For a quick dessert the kids will love, drizzle caramel ice cream topping over fresh apple slices.

1 package (16 ounces) frozen mixed vegetables

1 cup cut-up cooked chicken

1 jar (12 ounces) chicken gravy

2 cups shredded Cheddar cheese (8 ounces)

1 cup Original Bisquick mix

1/4 cup milk

1/4 cup dried thyme leaves

2 eggs

1 Heat oven to 375°. Heat vegetables, chicken and gravy to boiling in 2-quart saucepan, stirring frequently; keep warm.

2 Stir cheese, Bisquick mix, milk, thyme leaves and eggs with a fork until blended. Pour chicken mixture into ungreased 2-quart casserole. Pour batter over chicken mixture.

3 Bake 35 to 40 minutes or until crust is golden brown. Let stand 5 minutes before serving.

1 SERVING: Calories 400 (Calories from Fat 200); Fat 22g (Saturated 11g); Cholesterol 130mg; Sodium 920mg; Carbohydrate 27g (Dietary Fiber 4g); Protein 23g • % DAILY VALUE: Vitamin A 82%; Vitamin C 2%; Calcium 30%; Iron 22% • DIET EXCHANGES: 1 1/2 Starch, 1 Vegetable, 2 1/2 Medium-Fat Meat, 1 1/2 Fat • CARBOHYDRATE CHOICES: 2

Chicken Alfredo Pot Pie

prep: 20 min
bake: 30 min

I can (11 ounces) refrigerated soft breadsticks

I jar (16 ounces) Alfredo pasta sauce

1/3 cup milk

I bag (1 pound) frozen broccoli, cauli-flower and carrots, thawed and drained

2 cups cut-up cooked chicken

2 tablespoons grated Parmesan cheese

I teaspoon Italian seasoning

1 Heat oven to 375°. Unroll breadstick dough; separate at perforations to form 12 strips and set aside.

2 Mix pasta sauce, milk, vegetables and chicken in 3-quart saucepan. Heat to boiling, stirring occasionally. Spoon into ungreased rectangular pan, 13 × 9 × 2 inches.

3 Twist each dough strip; arrange crosswise over hot chicken mixture, gently stretching strips if necessary to fit. Sprinkle with cheese and Italian seasoning.

4 Bake uncovered 20 to 30 minutes or until breadsticks are deep golden brown.

wing it!

Serving this easy pot pie with crisp fresh veggies such as sliced red and green bell peppers, baby carrots, broccoli, cauliflower and celery sticks keeps the kids eating their veg-gies. Let the kids dip and dunk the veggies in the warm pie.

1 SERVING: Calories 520 (Calories from Fat 270); Fat 30g (Saturated 17g); Cholesterol 120mg; Sodium 730mg; Carbohydrate 36g (Dietary Fiber 4g); Protein 27g • % DAILY VALUE: Vitamin A 60%; Vitamin C 20%; Calcium 32%; Iron 14% • DIET EXCHANGES: 2 Starch, 1 Vegetable, 3 High-Fat Meat, 1 Fat • CARBOHYDRATE CHOICES: 2 1/2

Chicken and Corn Bread Stuffing Casserole

prep: **10 min**
bake: **40 min**

wing it!

Make a midweek dinner special. Serve this cozy casserole with a side of cranberry-orange relish or cranberry sauce.

1 can (10 3/4 ounces) condensed cream of chicken or celery soup

1 1/4 cups milk

1 cup frozen green peas

1/2 cup dried cranberries

4 medium green onions, sliced (1/4 cup)

2 cups cut-up cooked chicken

1 1/2 cups corn bread stuffing mix

1 cup Original Bisquick mix

1/4 cup milk

2 eggs

1 Heat oven to 400°. Grease 3-quart casserole. Heat soup and milk to boiling in 3-quart saucepan, stirring frequently. Stir in peas, cranberries and onions. Heat to boiling, stirring frequently; remove from heat. Stir in chicken and stuffing mix. Spoon into casserole.

2 Stir remaining ingredients until blended. Pour over stuffing mixture.

3 Bake uncovered 35 to 40 minutes or until knife inserted in center comes out clean.

1 SERVING: Calories 385 (Calories from Fat 115); Fat 13g (Saturated 4g); Cholesterol 120mg; Sodium 1030mg; Carbohydrate 45g (Dietary Fiber 3g); Protein 23g • % DAILY VALUE: Vitamin A 12%; Vitamin C 4%; Calcium 16%; Iron 16% • DIET EXCHANGES: 3 Starch, 2 Medium-Fat Meat • CARBOHYDRATE CHOICES: 3

Chicken and Corn Bread Stuffing Casserole

Chicken Enchiladas

wing **it!**

Who doesn't love enchiladas? Take this tasty dish to your next potluck and watch it disappear.

1 cup mild green sauce (salsa verde) or salsa

1/4 cup cilantro sprigs

1/4 cup parsley sprigs

1 tablespoon lime juice

2 cloves garlic

2 cups chopped cooked chicken

3/4 cup shredded mozzarella cheese (3 ounces)

6 flour tortillas (6 to 8 inches in diameter)

1 medium lime, cut into wedges

1 Heat oven to 350°. Spray rectangular baking dish, 11 × 7 × 1 1/2 inches, with cooking spray. Place green sauce, cilantro, parsley, lime juice and garlic in blender or food processor. Cover and blend on high speed about 30 seconds or until smooth. Reserve half of mixture.

2 Mix remaining sauce mixture, the chicken and 1/4 cup of the cheese. Spoon about 1/4 cup chicken mixture onto each tortilla. Roll tortilla around filling; place seam side down in baking dish.

3 Pour reserved sauce mixture over enchiladas. Sprinkle with remaining 1/2 cup cheese. Bake uncovered 20 to 25 minutes or until hot. Serve with lime wedges.

1 SERVING: Calories 275 (Calories from Fat 80); Fat 9g (Saturated 3g); Cholesterol 50mg; Sodium 510mg; Carbohydrate 28g (Dietary Fiber 2g); Protein 21g • % DAILY VALUE: Vitamin A 12%; Vitamin C 8%; Calcium 18%; Iron 14% • DIET EXCHANGES: 2 Starch, 2 Medium-Fat Meat • CARBOHYDRATE CHOICES: 2

Chicken and Green Beans with Rice

prep: 15 min
bake: 50 min

2 cups cut-up cooked chicken

2 cups cooked rice

1/2 teaspoon salt

1/4 teaspoon pepper

2 medium stalks celery, sliced (1 cup)

1 medium onion, chopped (1/2 cup)

1 can (14 1/2 ounces) ready-to-serve chicken broth

1 package (9 or 10 ounces) frozen cut green or yellow wax beans, thawed

1 Heat oven to 350°. Butter 2-quart casserole. Mix all ingredients in casserole.

2 Cover and bake 45 to 50 minutes or until beans are tender.

wing it!

This casserole is just about a meal in itself—just add a quick tossed salad and a yummy dessert. Why not serve make-your-own sundaes?

1 SERVING: Calories 185 (Calories from Fat 35); Fat 4g (Saturated 40g); Cholesterol 40mg; Sodium 545mg; Carbohydrate 20g (Dietary Fiber 2g); Protein 17g • % DAILY VALUE: Vitamin A 6%; Vitamin C 6%; Calcium 4%; Iron 10% • DIET EXCHANGES: 1 Starch, 1 Vegetable, 1 1/2 Lean Meat • CARBOHYDRATE CHOICES: 1

Chicken Noodle Casserole

prep: 20 min
bake: 45 min

1/4 cup uncooked egg noodles (8 ounces)

1 tablespoon vegetable oil

1 medium onion, chopped (1/2 cup)

2 medium stalks celery, sliced (1 cup)

3 cups cut-up cooked chicken

1/2 teaspoon salt

1/4 teaspoon pepper

1 can (14 1/2 ounces) ready-to-serve chicken broth

1 can (10 3/4 ounces) condensed cream of chicken soup

1 package (10 ounces) frozen green peas

1 can (4 ounces) sliced mushrooms, drained

1 Heat oven to 350°. Butter 3-quart casserole. Cook noodles as directed on package, except cook 2 minutes less than package directions.

2 While noodles are cooking, heat oil in 10-inch skillet over medium-high heat. Cook onion and celery in oil about 5 minutes, stirring occasionally, until tender. Stir in remaining ingredients.

3 Drain noodles; place in casserole. Top with chicken mixture. Cover and bake 30 minutes; stir. Bake uncovered about 15 minutes longer or until liquid is absorbed.

wing it!

To make this casserole ahead: Cover the baked casserole with aluminum foil. Freeze it no longer than 2 months. About 1 hour before serving, heat oven to 350°. Bake in covered casserole 45 minutes. Uncover and bake 10 to 15 minutes longer or until hot.

1 SERVING: Calories 280 (Calories from Fat 100); Fat 11g (Saturated 3g); Cholesterol 75mg; Sodium 910mg; Carbohydrate 27g (Dietary Fiber 4g); Protein 25g • **% DAILY VALUE:** Vitamin A 10%; Vitamin C 4%; Calcium 4%; Iron 20% • **DIET EXCHANGES:** 1 1/2 Starch, 1 Vegetable, 3 Lean Meat • **CARBOHYDRATE CHOICES:** 2

Cheesy Chicken Casserole

prep: 15 min
bake: 22 min

2 cups cut-up cooked chicken

1 jar (16 ounces) Cheddar cheese pasta sauce

1 bag (1 pound) frozen broccoli, carrots and cauliflower, thawed and drained

1 1/4 cups Original Bisquick mix

1/4 cup grated Parmesan cheese

1/4 cup firm butter or margarine

1 egg, slightly beaten

1 Heat oven to 400°. Mix chicken, pasta sauce and vegetables. Pour into ungreased square pan, 9 × 9 × 2 inches.

2 Mix Bisquick mix, Parmesan cheese and butter with fork or pastry blender until crumbly. Stir in egg. Sprinkle over chicken mixture.

3 Bake uncovered 20 to 22 minutes or until topping is light golden brown.

A 16-ounce jar of purchased Alfredo pasta sauce can be used in place of the Cheddar cheese sauce for a change of flavor.

1 SERVING: Calories 460 (Calories from Fat 260); Fat 29g (Saturated 14g); Cholesterol 130mg; Sodium 970mg; Carbohydrate 23g (Dietary Fiber 3g); Protein 27g • % DAILY VALUE: Vitamin A 60%; Vitamin C 20%; Calcium 34%; Iron 10% • DIET EXCHANGES: 1 Starch, 1 Vegetable, 3 Medium-Fat Meat, 3 Fat • CARBOHYDRATE CHOICES: 1 1/2

Cowboy Chicken and Beans

prep: **10 min**
bake: **40 min**

2 cups shredded cooked chicken

1/2 cup barbecue sauce

1 can (15 to 16 ounces) garbanzo beans, rinsed and drained

1 can (15 to 16 ounces) lima beans, rinsed and drained

1 can (15 to 16 ounces) kidney beans, rinsed and drained

1 cup shredded Cheddar cheese (4 ounces)

1 Heat oven to 350°. Spray 2-quart casserole with cooking spray. Mix chicken, barbecue sauce and beans in casserole.

2 Bake uncovered 30 to 35 minutes or until hot and bubbly. Sprinkle with cheese. Bake about 5 minutes longer or until cheese is melted.

wing it!

Let the kids make a zany zucchini cowboy head centerpiece for the table. Slice off one end of a large zucchini, and stand it on a plate. Decorate the top to look like a face, attaching food pieces such as carrot slices, raisins and grapes with toothpicks. Top it off with toy cowboy hat and bandana!

1 SERVING: Calories 495 (Calories from Fat 110); Fat 12g (Saturated 5g); Cholesterol 60mg; Sodium 1410mg; Carbohydrate 76g (Dietary Fiber 14g); Protein 34g • % DAILY VALUE: Vitamin A 8%; Vitamin C 4%; Calcium 20%; Iron 38% • DIET EXCHANGES: 5 Starch, 2 Lean Meat • CARBOHYDRATE CHOICES: 5

Chicken and Spinach Casserole

prep: **15 min**
bake: **20 min**

2 cups uncooked gemelli (twist) pasta (8 ounces)

1 package (1.8 ounces) leek soup mix

2 cups milk

1 cup cut-up cooked chicken

2 cups baby spinach leaves

1/4 cup freshly shredded Parmesan cheese

wing it!

Like some extra crunch? Just top with sliced toasted almonds or French-fried onions after baking.

1 Heat oven to 350°. Spray 1 1/2-quart casserole or square baking dish, 8 × 8 × 2 inches, with cooking spray. Cook and drain pasta as directed on package.

2 While pasta is cooking, mix soup mix (dry) and milk in 1-quart saucepan. Heat to boiling, stirring constantly.

3 Mix pasta, chicken and spinach in baking dish. Pour soup mixture over pasta mixture; stir gently to mix. Spread evenly. Sprinkle with cheese.

4 Bake uncovered about 20 minutes or until bubbly and light golden brown.

1 SERVING: Calories 410 (Calories from Fat 70); Fat 8g (Saturated 4g); Cholesterol 45mg; Sodium 1540mg; Carbohydrate 59g (Dietary Fiber 3g); Protein 25g • % DAILY VALUE: Vitamin A 34%; Vitamin C 8%; Calcium 28%; Iron 18% • DIET EXCHANGES: 3 Starch, 1 Milk, 1 Medium-Fat Meat • CARBOHYDRATE CHOICES: 4

Hot Chicken Salad with Sage Biscuits

prep: 20 min
bake: 20 min

wing it!

For an extra-special touch, sprinkle this warm salad with toasted sliced almonds and dried cranberries, and garnish with fresh sage leaves.

1/4 cup mayonnaise or salad dressing

2 tablespoons Original Bisquick mix

2 cups cut-up cooked chicken

1/4 cup shredded Cheddar cheese (1 ounce)

2 medium stalks celery, sliced (1 cup)

2 medium green onions, sliced (2 tablespoons)

2 1/4 cups Original Bisquick mix

3/4 cup milk

1/2 teaspoon dried sage leaves

1 Heat oven to 425°. Mix mayonnaise and 2 tablespoons Bisquick mix in medium bowl until well blended. Stir in chicken, cheese, celery and onions; set aside.

2 Mix remaining ingredients just until soft dough forms. Place on surface sprinkled with Bisquick mix; roll in Bisquick mix to coat. Shape into a ball; knead 10 times. Roll dough 1/2 inch thick. Cut with 1 1/2-inch round cutter dipped in Bisquick mix. Place close together around edge of ungreased 2-quart casserole.

3 Spoon chicken mixture into mound in center of biscuits. Bake uncovered 18 to 20 minutes or until biscuits are golden brown and chicken mixture is hot.

1 SERVING: Calories 370 (Calories from Fat 170); Fat 19g (Saturated 5g); Cholesterol 55mg; Sodium 820mg; Carbohydrate 31g (Dietary Fiber 1g); Protein 19g • % DAILY VALUE: Vitamin A 4%; Vitamin C 2%; Calcium 16%; Iron 12% • DIET EXCHANGES: 2 Starch, 2 Medium-Fat Meat, 1 1/2 Fat • CARBOHYDRATE CHOICES: 2

Hot Chicken Salad with Sage Biscuits

Impossibly Easy Chicken and Broccoli Pie

prep: **5 min**
bake: **35 min**
stand: **5 min**

wing it!

Looking for an easy way to sneak in some broccoli? The whole family will love this savory pie.

1 package (10 ounces) frozen chopped broccoli, thawed and drained

1 1/2 cups shredded Cheddar cheese (6 ounces)

1 cup cut-up cooked chicken

1 medium onion, chopped (1/2 cup)

1/2 cup Original Bisquick mix

1 cup milk

1/2 teaspoon salt

1/4 teaspoon pepper

2 eggs

1 Heat oven to 400°. Grease pie plate, 9 × 1 1/4 inches. Sprinkle broccoli, 1 cup of the cheese, the chicken and onion in pie plate.

2 Stir remaining ingredients until blended. Pour into pie plate.

3 Bake 30 to 35 minutes or until knife inserted in center comes out clean. Sprinkle with remaining 1/2 cup cheese. Bake 1 to 2 minutes or until cheese is melted. Let stand 5 minutes before serving.

1 SERVING: Calories 260 (Calories from Fat 135); Fat 15g (Saturated 8g); Cholesterol 125mg; Sodium 590mg; Carbohydrate 12g (Dietary Fiber 2g); Protein 19g • % DAILY VALUE: Vitamin A 24%; Vitamin C 14%; Calcium 24%; Iron 6% • DIET EXCHANGES: 1/2 Starch, 1 Vegetable, 2 1/2 Medium-Fat Meat • CARBOHYDRATE CHOICES: 1

Impossibly Easy Chicken and Broccoli Pie

prep: **20 min**
bake: **35 min**
stand: **5 min**

Impossibly Easy Chicken Club Pie

wing it!

Get a head start on your dinner by cooking the bacon, cutting up the chicken and shredding the cheese the night before. Enjoy an easy one-dish meal by topping the pie with shredded lettuce and sliced toma-toes. For dessert, serve fruit-yogurt smoothies.

1 1/2 cups cut-up cooked chicken

8 slices bacon, crisply cooked and crumbled

1 cup shredded Cheddar cheese (4 ounces)

1/2 cup Original or Reduced Fat Bisquick mix

1 cup milk

2 eggs

1 Heat oven to 400°. Spray bottom and side of pie plate, 9 × 1 1/4 inches, with cooking spray. Sprinkle chicken, bacon and cheese in pie plate.

2 Stir remaining ingredients until blended. Pour into pie plate.

3 Bake 30 to 35 minutes or until knife inserted in center comes out clean. Let stand 5 minutes before serving.

1 SERVING: Calories 275 (Calories from Fat 155); Fat 17g (Saturated 8g); Cholesterol 130mg; Sodium 410mg; Carbohydrate 8g (Dietary Fiber 0g); Protein 21g • **% DAILY VALUE:** Vitamin A 8%; Vitamin C 0%; Calcium 18%; Iron 6% • **DIET EXCHANGES:** 1/2 Starch, 3 Medium-Fat Meat • **CARBOHYDRATE CHOICES:** 1/2

Impossibly Easy Chicken Club Pie

prep: **5 min**
bake: **35 min**
stand: **5 min**

wing it!

Is company coming? Garnish each serving of this pie with a spoonful of warmed marinara or spaghetti sauce and a sprinkle of freshly shredded Parmesan cheese on top.

Impossibly Easy Chicken Primavera Pie

1 1/2 cups cut-up cooked chicken

1 package (10 ounces) frozen asparagus cuts, thawed and well drained

1 cup frozen stir-fry bell peppers and onions (from 1-pound bag), thawed and well drained

1/3 cup grated **Parmesan cheese**

1/2 cup **Original Bisquick mix**

1 cup milk

1/2 teaspoon salt

2 eggs

1 Heat oven to 400°. Grease pie plate, 9 × 1 1/4 inches. Layer chicken, asparagus, stir-fry mixture and cheese in pie plate.

2 Stir remaining ingredients until blended. Pour into pie plate.

3 Bake 30 to 35 minutes or until knife inserted in center comes out clean. Let stand 5 minutes before serving.

1 **SERVING**: Calories 200 (Calories from Fat 80); Fat 9g (Saturated 3g); Cholesterol 110mg; Sodium 580mg; Carbohydrate 12g (Dietary Fiber 1g); Protein 18g • **% DAILY VALUE**: Vitamin A 14%; Vitamin C 28%; Calcium 16%; Iron 8% • **DIET EXCHANGES**: 1/2 Starch, 1 Vegetable, 2 Medium-Fat Meat • **CARBOHYDRATE CHOICES**: 1

Impossibly Easy Chicken Primavera Pie

Roasted Chicken and Vegetable Egg Bake

prep: **20 min**
bake: **30 min**

wingit!

Other meal-starter vegetable blends are available with different vegetable combinations and seasonings. Any of them can be used in this recipe.

I tablespoon olive or vegetable oil

I large onion, chopped (1 cup)

I bag (26 ounces) frozen Parmesan herb-flavor oven-roasted potatoes, vegetables and cheese seasoning meal starter

I cup chopped cooked chicken

I cup Original Bisquick mix

I 1/2 cups milk

4 eggs

I cup shredded Italian-style cheese blend or mozzarella cheese (4 ounces)

1 Heat oven to 400°. Spray rectangular baking dish, 13 × 9 × 2 inches, with cooking spray. Heat oil in 12-inch nonstick skillet over medium heat. Cook onion and frozen vegetables in oil 8 to 10 minutes, stirring occasionally, until vegetables are heated through and crisp-tender. Add chicken and sprinkle vegetables with contents of seasoning packet from vegetables; stir gently to coat. Spread in baking dish.

2 Stir Bisquick mix, milk and eggs until blended. Pour over vegetables in baking dish.

3 Bake uncovered about 25 minutes or until knife inserted in center comes out clean. Sprinkle with cheese. Bake about 5 minutes or until cheese is melted.

1 SERVING: Calories 280 (Calories from Fat 100); Fat 11g (Saturated 4g); Cholesterol 130mg; Sodium 510mg; Carbohydrate 28g (Dietary Fiber 3g); Protein 17g • **% DAILY VALUE:** Vitamin A 20%; Vitamin C 18%; Calcium 22%; Iron 8% • **DIET EXCHANGES:** 1 1/2 Starch, 1 Vegetable, 1 1/2 Medium-Fat Meat, 1/2 Fat • **CARBOHYDRATE CHOICES:** 2

Roasted Chicken and Vegetable Egg Bake

Tuscan Chicken Torta

prep: **15 min**
bake: **55 min**
stand: **10 min**

wing it!

**Cannellini beans
are large, white
Italian kidney
beans. They are
particularly popu-
lar in soups and
salads, but in this
recipe, they are
mashed to make
a delicious crust.**

I can (15 to 16 ounces) cannellini
beans, rinsed and drained

I 1/3 cups Original Bisquick mix

1/3 cup Italian dressing

1 1/2 cups diced cooked chicken

1 package (10 ounces) frozen chopped
spinach, thawed and squeezed to drain

1 cup shredded mozzarella cheese
(4 ounces)

3 eggs

1 1/4 cups milk

1/3 cup slivered almonds, toasted

1 Heat oven to 375°. Mash beans in medium bowl. Stir in Bisquick mix
and dressing. Spread in bottom and 2 inches up side of ungreased spring-
form pan, 9 × 3 inches. Bake 10 to 12 minutes or until set.

2 Layer chicken, spinach and cheese over crust. Mix eggs and milk; pour
over cheese. Sprinkle almonds evenly over top.

3 Bake uncovered 50 to 55 minutes or until golden brown and knife
inserted near center comes out clean. Let stand 10 minutes. Loosen edge
of torta from side of pan; remove side of pan.

1 SERVING: Calories 465 (Calories from Fat 205); Fat 23g (Saturated 6g); Cholesterol 150mg;
Sodium 800mg; Carbohydrate 41g (Dietary Fiber 7g); Protein 30g • **% DAILY VALUE:** Vitamin A 62%;
Vitamin C 4%; Calcium 36%; Iron 22% • **DIET EXCHANGES:** 2 1/2 Starch, 1 Vegetable, 3 Medium-Fat Meat,
1/2 Fat • **CARBOHYDRATE CHOICES:** 3

Wild Rice and Chicken Casserole

prep: 15 min
bake: 1 hr 5 min

2 cups cut-up cooked chicken

2 1/4 cups boiling water

1/3 cup skim milk

1 small onion, chopped (1/4 cup)

1 can (10 3/4 ounces) condensed cream of mushroom soup

1 package (6.2 ounces) fast-cooking long grain and wild rice mix

1 Heat oven to 350°. Mix all ingredients, including contents of seasoning packet from rice mix, in ungreased 2-quart casserole.

2 Cover and bake 45 to 50 minutes or until rice is tender. Uncover and bake 10 to 15 minutes longer or until liquid is absorbed.

wing it!

This dish is a great way to use up those leftovers. If you like, toss in chopped vegetables, such as carrots or celery, for a healthy and hearty one-dish meal.

1 SERVING: Calories 245 (Calories from Fat 65); Fat 7g (Saturated 2g); Cholesterol 40mg; Sodium 400mg; Carbohydrate 27g (Dietary Fiber 2g); Protein 19g • % DAILY VALUE: Vitamin A 0%; Vitamin C 0%; Calcium 4%; Iron 8% • DIET EXCHANGES: 1 1/2 Starch, 2 Lean Meat • CARBOHYDRATE CHOICES: 2

Chicken Garden Vegetable Bake

prep: **20 min**
bake: **35 min**
stand: **5 min**

wing it!

The farmers' market is a great place to look for fresh vegetables. Or instead of the zucchini, use 1 cup green peas, chopped broccoli or 1-inch asparagus pieces.

1/2 cup grated reduced-fat Parmesan cheese topping

1 cup chopped zucchini

2/3 cup drained canned whole kernel corn

1 small tomato, chopped (1/2 cup)

1 medium onion, chopped (1/2 cup)

1 cup cut-up cooked chicken

3/4 cup Original or Reduced Fat Bisquick mix

1 cup fat-free (skim) milk

2 eggs or 4 egg whites

1/2 teaspoon salt

1/4 teaspoon pepper

1 Heat oven to 400°. Spray square baking dish, $8 \times 8 \times 2$ inches, with cooking spray. Sprinkle 1/4 cup of the cheese in baking dish. Top with zucchini, corn, tomato, onion and chicken. Sprinkle remaining 1/4 cup cheese over vegetables.

2 Stir remaining ingredients until blended. Pour over vegetables and cheese.

3 Bake uncovered 32 to 35 minutes or until knife inserted in center comes out clean. Let stand 5 minutes before cutting.

1 **SERVING:** Calories 205 (Calories from Fat 65); Fat 7g (Saturated 2g); Cholesterol 95mg; Sodium 660mg; Carbohydrate 21g (Dietary Fiber 1g); Protein 14g • **% DAILY VALUE:** Vitamin A 10%; Vitamin C 6%; Calcium 14%; Iron 8% • **DIET EXCHANGES:** 1 Starch, 1 Vegetable, 1 Medium-Fat Meat, 1/2 Fat • **CARBOHYDRATE CHOICES:** 1 1/2

7 Main Dish Magic

= **super express** ready in 20 minutes or less

Chicken à la King

prep: 25 min
cook: 10 min

1/2 cup butter or margarine

1 small green bell pepper, chopped (1/2 cup)

1 cup sliced mushrooms (3 ounces)

1/2 cup all-purpose flour

1/2 teaspoon salt

1/4 teaspoon pepper

1 1/2 cups milk

1 1/4 cups ready-to-serve chicken broth

2 cups cut-up cooked chicken

1 jar (2 ounces) diced pimientos, drained

12 toasted bread triangles or 3 cups hot cooked rice

1 Melt butter in 3-quart saucepan over medium-high heat. Cook bell pepper and mushrooms in butter, stirring occasionally, until bell pepper is crisp-tender.

2 Stir in flour, salt and pepper. Cook over medium heat, stirring constantly, until bubbly; remove from heat. Stir in milk and broth. Heat to boiling, stirring constantly. Boil and stir 1 minute.

3 Stir in chicken and pimientos; cook until hot. Serve over toasted bread triangles.

wing it!

Instead of using fresh mushrooms, you can use a 4-ounce can of mushroom pieces and stems, drained. For a little extra flavor, save the mushroom liquid and use it as part of the milk.

1 SERVING: Calories 375 (Calories from Fat 190); Fat 21g (Saturated 5g); Cholesterol 45mg; Sodium 790mg; Carbohydrate 26g (Dietary Fiber 1g); Protein 20g • % DAILY VALUE: Vitamin A 24%; Vitamin C 16%; Calcium 12%; Iron 12% • DIET EXCHANGES: 1 1/2 Starch, 1 Vegetable, 2 Medium-Fat Meat, 2 Fat • CARBOHYDRATE CHOICES: 2

Chicken à la King

Chicken and Dumplings

prep: **5 min**
cook: **25 min**

wing it!

Keep your dumplings tender by not over-mixing the dough. Mix it just until moistened and then resist the urge to keep on going.

1 1/2 cups milk

1 cup frozen peas and carrots

1 cup cut-up cooked chicken

1 can (10 3/4 ounces) condensed cream of chicken and mushroom soup

1 cup Original Bisquick mix

1/3 cup milk

Paprika, if desired

1 Heat 1 1/2 cups milk, the peas and carrots, chicken and soup to boiling in 3-quart saucepan.

2 Stir Bisquick mix and 1/3 cup milk until soft dough forms. Drop dough by 8 spoonfuls onto chicken mixture; reduce heat to low.

3 Cook uncovered 10 minutes. Cover and cook 10 minutes longer. Sprinkle with paprika.

1 SERVING: Calories 335 (Calories from Fat 125); Fat 14g (Saturated 5g); Cholesterol 45mg; Sodium 1080mg; Carbohydrate 34g (Dietary Fiber 2g); Protein 19g • % DAILY VALUE: Vitamin A 84%; Vitamin C 2%; Calcium 20%; Iron 12% • DIET EXCHANGES: 2 Starch, 2 Medium-Fat Meat, 1/2 Fat • CARBOHYDRATE CHOICES: 2

Chicken and Dumplings

Chicken Divan

prep: **40 min**
broil: **3 min**

wing it!

Use two packages
(10 ounces each)
frozen broccoli
spears, cooked
and drained, for
the fresh broccoli
to save time.

I 1/2 pounds broccoli

1/4 cup butter or margarine

1/4 cup all-purpose flour

1/8 teaspoon ground nutmeg

I 1/2 cups ready-to-serve chicken broth

I cup grated Parmesan cheese

1/2 cup whipping (heavy) cream

2 tablespoons dry white wine or ready-to-serve chicken broth

6 large slices cooked chicken breast, 1/4 inch thick

1 Cut broccoli lengthwise into 1/2-inch-wide spears. Heat 1 inch water (salted if desired) to boiling in 2-quart saucepan. Add broccoli. Heat to boiling. Boil uncovered 5 minutes; drain. Remove broccoli from saucepan.

2 Melt butter in same saucepan over medium heat. Stir in flour and nutmeg. Cook, stirring constantly, until smooth and bubbly; remove from heat. Gradually stir in broth. Heat to boiling, stirring constantly. Boil and stir 1 minute; remove from heat. Stir in 1/2 cup of the cheese, the whipping cream and wine.

3 Place broccoli in ungreased rectangular baking dish, 11 × 7 × 1 1/2 inches. Top with chicken. Pour cheese sauce over chicken. Sprinkle with remaining 1/2 cup cheese.

4 Set oven control to broil. Broil with top 3 to 5 inches from heat about 3 minutes or until cheese is bubbly and light brown.

1 SERVING: Calories 350 (Calories from Fat 200); Fat 32g (Saturated 13g); Cholesterol 105mg; Sodium 690mg; Carbohydrate 9g (Dietary Fiber 2g); Protein 29g • **% DAILY VALUE:** Vitamin A 30%; Vitamin C 54%; Calcium 28%; Iron 10% • **DIET EXCHANGES:** 2 Vegetable, 3 1/2 Medium-Fat Meat, 2 1/2 Fat • **CARBOHYDRATE CHOICES:** 1/2

Chicken Thermidor

prep: 15 min
cook: 15 min

1 1/2 cups sliced mushrooms (4 ounces)

2 large shallots or 1 small onion, finely chopped (1/4 cup)

2 tablespoons all-purpose flour

1 teaspoon chicken bouillon granules

1 1/4 cups fat-free half-and-half or refrigerated fat-free nondairy creamer

1 1/2 cups cut-up cooked chicken

2 tablespoons dry white wine or ready-to-serve chicken broth

1/2 teaspoon dried tarragon leaves

4 slices white or whole wheat bread, toasted and cut into fourths, or 2 English muffins, split, toasted and cut into fourths

Grated Parmesan cheese, if desired

1 Spray 2-quart saucepan with cooking spray; heat over medium heat. Cook mushrooms and shallots in saucepan about 5 minutes, stirring frequently, until mushrooms are tender. Stir in flour and bouillon granules. Cook over medium heat, stirring constantly, until mixture is bubbly; remove from heat.

2 Gradually stir in half-and-half. Heat to boiling, stirring constantly. Boil and stir 1 minute. Stir in chicken, wine and tarragon; reduce heat to low. Cook about 5 minutes, stirring occasionally, until heated through. Spoon over toast. Sprinkle with cheese.

wing it !

By using chicken instead of lobster, fat-free half-and-half in place of rich cream and no butter for sautéing, classic Lobster Thermidor is transformed into this exquisite, good-for-you entrée.

1 SERVING: Calories 245 (Calories from Fat 55); Fat 6g (Saturated 1g); Cholesterol 45mg; Sodium 510mg; Carbohydrate 28g (Dietary Fiber 1g); Protein 19g • % DAILY VALUE: Vitamin A 2%; Vitamin C 2%; Calcium 4%; Iron 12% • DIET EXCHANGES: 1 Starch, 1 Vegetable, 1/2 Milk, 1 1/2 Medium-Fat Meat • CARBOHYDRATE CHOICES: 2

Chicken Paprika

prep: 15 min
cook: 12 min

wing it!

This updated version of Chicken Paprikash allows you to enjoy all the traditional spicy flavor of the dish with less fat and sodium and fewer calories than old-time recipes. For a touch of authenticity, use fiery Hungarian paprika, but use only 1 tablespoon to start and then add more to taste.

2 medium onions, cut lengthwise in half, then cut crosswise into very thin slices

2 medium stalks celery, sliced (1 cup)

4 cloves garlic, finely chopped

2 tablespoons paprika

1/4 teaspoon pepper

1 1/2 cups cut-up cooked chicken

1/2 cup ready-to-serve chicken broth

1 cup reduced-fat sour cream

Hot cooked wide egg noodles, if desired

Chopped fresh parsley, if desired

1 Spray 10-inch nonstick skillet with cooking spray; heat over medium heat. Cook onions, celery and garlic in skillet about 5 minutes, stirring frequently, until onions are tender. Stir in paprika and pepper. Cook 1 minute, stirring constantly.

2 Stir in chicken and broth. Heat to boiling; reduce heat to medium. Stir sour cream into liquid in skillet. Heat over medium heat just until heated through. Serve over noodles. Sprinkle with parsley.

1 SERVING: Calories 220 (Calories from Fat 100); Fat 11g (Saturated 6g); Cholesterol 65mg; Sodium 220mg; Carbohydrate 11g (Dietary Fiber 2g); Protein 19g • % DAILY VALUE: Vitamin A 52%; Vitamin C 6%; Calcium 10%; Iron 10% • DIET EXCHANGES: 1/2 Starch, 1 Vegetable, 2 Medium-Fat Meat • CARBOHYDRATE CHOICES: 1

Chicken Paprika

prep: 10 min
cook: 8 min

wingit!

When you have only minutes to rustle up dinner, this quick-cooking chicken-and-couscous medley can be a lifesaver.

4 SERVINGS

Chicken with Roasted Peppers and Couscous

1 can (14 1/2 ounces) ready-to-serve chicken broth

1 package (10 ounces) frozen whole kernel corn, thawed

1 1/2 cups cubed cooked chicken

1 1/4 cups uncooked couscous

1 jar (7 1/4 ounces) roasted red bell peppers, drained and coarsely chopped

1 Heat broth and corn to boiling in 3-quart saucepan; reduce heat to low. Stir in remaining ingredients.

2 Cover and simmer about 3 minutes, stirring occasionally, until couscous is tender and chicken is heated through.

1 **SERVING:** Calories 380 (Calories from Fat 45); Fat 5g (Saturated 1g); Cholesterol 45mg; Sodium 490mg; Carbohydrate 58g (Dietary Fiber 5g); Protein 26g • % **DAILY VALUE:** Vitamin A 54%; Vitamin C 50%; Calcium 2%; Iron 10% • **DIET EXCHANGES:** 4 Starch, 2 Very Lean Meat • **CARBOHYDRATE CHOICES:** 4

Chicken with Roasted Peppers and Couscous

prep: 15 min
cook: 5 min

wing it!

Round this meal out with an easy, low-fat dessert. Slice a purchased angel food cake loaf into slices. Top with berries or sliced fruit such as peaches or nectarines.

4 SERVINGS

Easy Curried Chicken and Couscous

1 3/4 cups water

1 cup uncooked couscous

1 can (10 3/4 ounces) condensed reduced-fat cream of chicken soup

1/2 cup water

1 1/2 teaspoons curry powder

1 1/2 cups cut-up cooked chicken

2 cups frozen mixed vegetables, thawed

1 Heat 1 3/4 cups water to boiling in 10-inch nonstick skillet. Stir in couscous; remove from heat. Cover and let stand about 5 minutes or until water is absorbed. Remove couscous to large serving platter; keep warm.

2 Heat soup, 1/2 cup water, the curry powder, chicken and vegetables to boiling in same skillet; reduce heat. Cover and simmer 3 to 5 minutes or until vegetables are tender. Pour chicken mixture over couscous.

1 SERVING: Calories 370 (Calories from Fat 65); Fat 7g (Saturated 2g); Cholesterol 50mg; Sodium 670mg; Carbohydrate 51g (Dietary Fiber 6g); Protein 25g • % DAILY VALUE: Vitamin A 84%; Vitamin C 2%; Calcium 4%; Iron 12% • DIET EXCHANGES: 3 Starch, 1 Vegetable, 1 1/2 Lean Meat • CARBOHYDRATE CHOICES: 3 1/2

4 SERVINGS

Easy Mexican Chicken and Beans

prep: 10 min
cook: 10 min

2 cups cooked chicken breast, cut into strips

1 envelope (1 1/4 ounces) taco seasoning mix

1 can (15 to 16 ounces) black or pinto beans, rinsed and drained

1 can (11 ounces) whole kernel corn with red and green peppers, undrained

1/4 cup water

Turn this dish into a weeknight fiesta! Serve with flour tortillas, sour cream, salsa, black olives and green chiles and let everyone make their own wrap.

1 Mix together all ingredients in 2-quart saucepan.

2 Cook over medium-high heat 8 to 10 minutes, stirring frequently, until sauce is slightly thickened.

1 **SERVING:** Calories 355 (Calories from Fat 70); Fat 8g (Saturated 2g); Cholesterol 75mg; Sodium 950mg; Carbohydrate 44g (Dietary Fiber 8g); Protein 35g • % **DAILY VALUE:** Vitamin A 16%; Vitamin C 8%; Calcium 10%; Iron 24% • **DIET EXCHANGES:** 3 Starch, 3 Very Lean Meat • **CARBOHYDRATE CHOICES:** 3

Fiesta Chicken and Rice

prep: 10 min
cook: 25 min

wing it!

Like it hot? Go ahead and add a few drops of red pepper sauce to increase the heat.

I 1/4 cups water

I can (5 1/2 ounces) spicy eight-vegetable juice

I package (4.9 ounces) rice and vermicelli mix with chicken broth and broccoli

I 1/2 cups cubed cooked chicken

I cup frozen chopped bell peppers (from 10-ounce bag), thawed

1 Heat water, vegetable juice, rice-vermicelli mix and seasoning packet to boiling in 3-quart saucepan, stirring occasionally; reduce heat.

2 Simmer covered 15 to 20 minutes, stirring occasionally. Stir in chicken and bell peppers; heat through.

1 SERVING: Calories 165 (Calories from Fat 45); Fat 5g (Saturated 1g); Cholesterol 45mg; Sodium 300mg; Carbohydrate 13g (Dietary Fiber 1g); Protein 17g • **% DAILY VALUE:** Vitamin A 16%; Vitamin C 36%; Calcium 2%; Iron 6% • **DIET EXCHANGES:** 1 Starch, 2 Very Lean Meat • **CARBOHYDRATE CHOICES:** 1

Creamy Chicken and Vegetables with Noodles

prep: 15 min
cook: 8 min

5 cups uncooked medium noodles (10 ounces)

2 cups frozen mixed vegetables, thawed

6 medium green onions, sliced (6 tablespoons)

1 tub (8 ounces) garden vegetable fat-free cream cheese

1 1/4 cups skim milk

1 1/2 cups cut-up cooked chicken

1/2 teaspoon garlic salt

1/4 teaspoon pepper

Chopped fresh parsley, if desired

wing it!

Using chicken breast in this colorful meal-in-a-skillet helps keep it lower in fat and calories than if you made it with dark meat.

1 Cook noodles as directed on package. While noodles are cooking, spray 12-inch nonstick skillet with cooking spray; heat over medium heat. Cook vegetables and onions in skillet about 4 minutes, stirring frequently, until vegetables are crisp-tender.

2 Stir cream cheese and milk into vegetable mixture until blended. Stir in chicken, garlic salt and pepper; heat through.

3 Drain noodles. Stir noodles into cheese sauce mixture; heat through. Sprinkle with parsley.

1 SERVING: Calories 460 (Calories from Fat 70); Fat 8g (Saturated 2g); Cholesterol 110mg; Sodium 560mg; Carbohydrate 67g (Dietary Fiber 7g); Protein 37g • **% DAILY VALUE:** Vitamin A 98%; Vitamin C 6%; Calcium 26%; Iron 26% • **DIET EXCHANGES:** 4 Starch, 1 Vegetable, 3 Very Lean Meat • **CARBOHYDRATE CHOICES:** 4 1/2

Everyday Chicken Risotto

prep: **10 min**
cook: **30 min**

wing it!

Risotto is on every Italian restaurant menu, and now you can make it easily at home!

2 tablespoons olive or vegetable oil

1/3 cup chopped green onions

1 medium carrot, thinly sliced (1/2 cup)

2 cloves garlic, finely chopped

1 cup uncooked Arborio or regular long-grain rice

3 1/2 cups ready-to-serve chicken broth

1 tablespoon chopped fresh parsley

1/8 teaspoon saffron threads, crushed, or ground turmeric

2 cups cut-up cooked chicken

1 Heat oil in 3-quart saucepan over medium-high heat. Cook onions, carrot and garlic in oil about 4 to 5 minutes, stirring frequently, until carrots are crisp-tender. Stir in rice. Cook, stirring frequently, until rice begins to brown.

2 Pour 1/2 cup broth, parsley and saffron over rice. Cook uncovered, stirring occasionally, until liquid is absorbed. Continue cooking 15 to 20 minutes, adding broth 1/2 cup at a time and stirring occasionally, until rice is tender and creamy. Stir in chicken; heat through.

1 **SERVING:** Calories 275 (Calories from Fat 80); Fat 9g (Saturated 2g); Cholesterol 40mg; Sodium 640mg; Carbohydrate 29g (Dietary Fiber 1g); Protein 19g • **% DAILY VALUE:** Vitamin A 38%; Vitamin C 2%; Calcium 2%; Iron 12% • **DIET EXCHANGES:** 2 Starch, 2 Lean Meat • **CARBOHYDRATE CHOICES:** 2

Everyday Chicken Risotto

prep: **10 min**
cook: **10 min**

wing it!

Some say that jambalaya—a classic Creole dish—got its name from the French word for ham (*jambon*), which was the main ingredient in many of the first jambalayas. Using chicken in this recipe is just one of the many variations on the jambalaya theme.

4 SERVINGS

Slim and Trim Jambalaya

1 bag (16 ounces) frozen small whole onions, thawed

1 can (14 1/2 ounces) ready-to-serve chicken broth

1 can (14 1/2 ounces) chunky chili tomato sauce or regular tomato sauce

1 1/2 cups cubed cooked chicken

1 1/2 cups uncooked instant rice

1 Heat onions, broth and tomato sauce to boiling in 3-quart saucepan, stirring occasionally; reduce heat.

2 Stir in chicken and rice; reduce heat to low. Cover and cook about 5 minutes, stirring occasionally, until rice is tender and chicken is heated through.

1 **SERVING:** Calories 385 (Calories from Fat 80); Fat 9g (Saturated 2g); Cholesterol 45mg; Sodium 850mg; Carbohydrate 53g (Dietary Fiber 4g); Protein 23g • % **DAILY VALUE:** Vitamin A 18%; Vitamin C 24%; Calcium 8%; Iron 18% • **DIET EXCHANGES:** 3 Starch, 1 Vegetable, 2 Lean Meat • **CARBOHYDRATE CHOICES:** 3 1/2

Sweet-and-Sour Chicken Crepes

prep: **25 min**
cook: **6 min**

Crepes (below)

2 cups frozen stir-fry bell peppers and onions (from 1-pound bag), thawed and drained

1 cup cut-up cooked chicken

1 can (8 ounces) pineapple tidbits or chunks, drained

2/3 cup sweet-and-sour sauce

1 Make Crepes.

2 Heat stir-fry vegetables, chicken, pineapple and 1/3 cup of the sweet-and-sour sauce in 2-quart saucepan over medium-high heat about 5 minutes, stirring constantly, until hot.

3 Spoon about 2 tablespoons filling onto each crepe. Roll up; carefully place seam side down. Heat remaining 1/3 cup sweet-and-sour sauce until hot. Serve over crepes.

Crepes

1 cup Original Bisquick mix

3/4 cup milk

1 teaspoon soy sauce

1 egg

1 Stir all ingredients until blended. Lightly spray 6- or 7-inch skillet with cooking spray; heat over medium-high heat.

2 For each crepe, pour 2 tablespoons batter into hot skillet; rotate skillet until batter covers bottom. Cook until golden brown. Gently loosen edge with metal spatula; turn and cook other side until golden brown.

3 Stack crepes as you remove them from skillet, placing waxed paper between each. Keep crepes covered to prevent them from drying out.

wing it!

Make the crepes ahead of time. Place the stack of crepes in a resealable plastic bag and refrigerate. At suppertime, make the filling and quickly reheat the crepes in the microwave on High for 30 seconds. Assemble and serve.

1 **SERVING:** Calories 345 (Calories from Fat 110); Fat 12g (Saturated 3g); Cholesterol 85mg; Sodium 910mg; Carbohydrate 43g (Dietary Fiber 2g); Protein 16g • % **DAILY VALUE:** Vitamin A 10%; Vitamin C 46%; Calcium 14%; Iron 12% • **DIET EXCHANGES:** 2 Starch, 1/2 Fruit, 1 Vegetable, 1 Medium-Fat Meat, 1 Fat • **CARBOHYDRATE CHOICES:** 3

prep: **10 min**
cook: **7 min**

4 SERVINGS

Vegetable-Chicken Stir-Fry

1 tablespoons vegetable oil

3 cups cut-up assorted vegetables (bell peppers, broccoli flowerets, shredded carrots)

1 clove garlic, finely chopped

2 cups cubed chicken

1/2 cup stir-fry sauce

1 Heat 1 tablespoon of the oil in 12-inch skillet or wok over high heat.

2 Add vegetables and garlic; stir-fry about 2 minutes or until vegetables are crisp-tender. Add chicken and stir-fry sauce. Cook and stir about 2 minutes or until hot.

1 SERVING: Calories 295 (Calories from Fat 110); Fat 12g (Saturated 3g); Cholesterol 100mg; Sodium 1500mg; Carbohydrate 10g (Dietary Fiber 2g); Protein 37g • **% DAILY VALUE:** Vitamin A 40%; Vitamin C 20%; Calcium 4%; Iron 12% • **DIET EXCHANGES:** 2 Vegetable, 4 1/2 Lean Meat • **CARBOHYDRATE CHOICES:** 1/2

Vegetable-Chicken Stir-Fry

Helpful Nutrition and Cooking Information

Nutrition Guidelines

We provide nutrition information for each recipe that includes calories, fat, cholesterol, sodium, carbohydrate, fiber and protein. Individual food choices can be based on this information.

Recommended intake for a daily diet of 2,000 calories as set by the Food and Drug Administration

Total Fat	**Less than 65g**
Saturated Fat	**Less than 20g**
Cholesterol	**Less than 300mg**
Sodium	**Less than 2,400mg**
Total Carbohydrate	**300g**
Dietary Fiber	**25g**

Criteria Used for Calculating Nutrition Information

- The first ingredient was used wherever a choice is given (such as 1/3 cup sour cream or plain yogurt).
- The first ingredient amount was used wherever a range is given (such as 3- to 3-1/2–pound cut-up broiler-fryer chicken).
- The first serving number was used wherever a range is given (such as 4 to 6 servings).
- "If desired" ingredients and recipe variations were not included (such as sprinkle with brown sugar, if desired).
- Only the amount of a marinade or frying oil that is estimated to be absorbed by the food during preparation or cooking was calculated.

Ingredients Used in Recipe Testing and Nutrition Calculations

- Ingredients used for testing represent those that the majority of consumers use in their homes: large eggs, 2% milk, 80%-lean ground beef, canned ready-to-use chicken broth and vegetable oil spread containing not less than 65 percent fat.
- Fat-free, low-fat or low-sodium products were not used, unless otherwise indicated.
- Solid vegetable shortening (not butter, margarine, nonstick cooking sprays or vegetable oil spread as they can cause sticking problems) was used to grease pans, unless otherwise indicated.

Equipment Used in Recipe Testing

We use equipment for testing that the majority of consumers use in their homes. If a specific piece of equipment (such as a wire whisk) is necessary for recipe success, it is listed in the recipe.

- Cookware and bakeware without nonstick coatings were used, unless otherwise indicated.
- No dark-colored, black or insulated bakeware was used.
- When a pan is specified in a recipe, a metal pan was used; a baking dish or pie plate means ovenproof glass was used.
- An electric hand mixer was used for mixing only when mixer speeds are specified in the recipe directions. When a mixer speed is not given, a spoon or fork was used.

Cooking Terms Glossary

Beat: Mix ingredients vigorously with spoon, fork, wire whisk, hand beater or electric mixer until smooth and uniform.

Boil: Heat liquid until bubbles rise continuously and break on the surface and steam is given off. For rolling boil, the bubbles form rapidly.

Chop: Cut into coarse or fine irregular pieces with a knife, food chopper, blender or food processor.

Cube: Cut into squares 1/2 inch or larger.

Dice: Cut into squares smaller than 1/2 inch.

Grate: Cut into tiny particles using small rough holes of grater (citrus peel or chocolate).

Grease: Rub the inside surface of a pan with shortening, using pastry brush, piece of waxed paper or paper towel, to prevent food from sticking during baking (as for some casseroles).

Julienne: Cut into thin, matchlike strips, using knife or food processor (vegetables, fruits, meats).

Mix: Combine ingredients in any way that distributes them evenly.

Sauté: Cook foods in hot oil or margarine over medium-high heat with frequent tossing and turning motion.

Shred: Cut into long thin pieces by rubbing food across the holes of a shredder, as for cheese, or by using a knife to slice very thinly, as for cabbage.

Simmer: Cook in liquid just below the boiling point on top of the stove; usually after reducing heat from a boil. Bubbles will rise slowly and break just below the surface.

Stir: Mix ingredients until uniform consistency. Stir once in a while for stirring occasionally, often for stirring frequently and continuously for stirring constantly.

Toss: Tumble ingredients (such as green salad) lightly with a lifting motion, usually to coat evenly or mix with another food.

metric conversion chart

Volume

U.S. Units	Canadian Metric	Australian Metric
1/4 teaspoon	1 mL	1 ml
1/2 teaspoon	2 mL	2 ml
1 teaspoon	5 mL	5 ml
1 tablespoon	15 mL	20 ml
1/4 cup	50 mL	60 ml
1/3 cup	75 mL	80 ml
1/2 cup	125 mL	125 ml
2/3 cup	150 mL	170 ml
3/4 cup	175 mL	190 ml
1 cup	250 mL	250 ml
1 quart	1 liter	1 liter
1 1/2 quarts	1.5 liters	1.5 liters
2 quarts	2 liters	2 liters
2 1/2 quarts	2.5 liters	2.5 liters
3 quarts	3 liters	3 liters
4 quarts	4 liters	4 liters

Measurements

Inches	Centimeters
1	2.5
2	5.0
3	7.5
4	10.0
5	12.5
6	15.0
7	17.5
8	20.5
9	23.0
10	25.5
11	28.0
12	30.5
13	33.0

Temperatures

Fahrenheit	Celsius
32°	0°
212°	100°
250°	120°
275°	140°
300°	150°
325°	160°
350°	180°
375°	190°
400°	200°
425°	220°
450°	230°
475°	240°
500°	260°

Weight

U.S. Units	Canadian Metric	Australian Metric
1 ounce	30 grams	30 grams
2 ounces	55 grams	60 grams
3 ounces	85 grams	90 grams
4 ounces (1/4 pound)	115 grams	125 grams
8 ounces (1/2 pound)	225 grams	225 grams
16 ounces (1 pound)	455 grams	500 grams
1 pound	455 grams	1/2 kilogram

Note: The recipes in this cookbook have not been developed or tested using metric measures. When converting recipes to metric, some variations in quality may be noted.

Index

Page numbers in *italic* indicate illustrations

Complete your cookbook library
with these *Betty Crocker* titles

Betty Crocker's Best Bread Machine Cookbook
Betty Crocker's Best Chicken Cookbook
Betty Crocker's Best Christmas Cookbook
Betty Crocker's Best of Baking
Betty Crocker's Best of Healthy and Hearty Cooking
Betty Crocker's Best-Loved Recipes
Betty Crocker's Bisquick® Cookbook
Betty Crocker Bisquick® II Cookbook
Betty Crocker Bisquick® Impossibly Easy Pies
Betty Crocker Celebrate!
Betty Crocker's Complete Thanksgiving Cookbook
Betty Crocker's Cook Book for Boys and Girls
Betty Crocker's Cook It Quick
Betty Crocker's Cookbook, 9th Edition— *The* **BIG RED** *Cookbook*®
Betty Crocker's Cookbook, Bridal Edition
Betty Crocker's Cookie Book
Betty Crocker's Cooking Basics
Betty Crocker's Cooking for Two
Betty Crocker's Cooky Book, Facsimile Edition
Betty Crocker's Diabetes Cookbook
Betty Crocker's Easy Slow Cooker Dinners
Betty Crocker's Eat and Lose Weight
Betty Crocker's Entertaining Basics
Betty Crocker's Flavors of Home
Betty Crocker 4-Ingredient Dinners
Betty Crocker's Great Grilling
Betty Crocker's Healthy New Choices
Betty Crocker's Indian Home Cooking
Betty Crocker's Italian Cooking
Betty Crocker's Kids Cook!
Betty Crocker's Kitchen Library
Betty Crocker's Living with Cancer Cookbook
Betty Crocker's Low-Fat, Low-Cholesterol Cooking Today
Betty Crocker More Slow Cooker Recipes
Betty Crocker's New Cake Decorating
Betty Crocker's New Chinese Cookbook
Betty Crocker's A Passion for Pasta
Betty Crocker's Pasta Favorites
Betty Crocker's Picture Cook Book, Facsimile Edition
Betty Crocker's Quick & Easy Cookbook
Betty Crocker's Slow Cooker Cookbook
Betty Crocker's Ultimate Cake Mix Cookbook
Betty Crocker's Vegetarian Cooking